Stephen Page

Transport for tourism

London and New York

First published 1994
by Routledge
11 New Fetter Lane, London EC4P 4EE

Simultaneously published in the USA and Canada
by Routledge
29 West 35th Street, New York, NY 10001

Typeset in Times by Florencetype Ltd, Stoodleigh, Devon
Printed and bound in Great Britain by
Biddles Ltd, Guildford and King's Lynn

British Library Cataloguing in Publication Data
A catalogue record for this book is available from the
British Library.

Library of Congress Cataloging in Publication Data
Page, Stephen, 1963–
    Transport for tourism/Stephen Page.
    p. cm. – (Routledge topics in tourism)
    Includes bibliographical references.
    1. Tourist trade. 2. Transportation. I. Title. II. Series.
    G155.A1P26 1994
    338.4′791–dc20   93–39536
                                                              CIP

ISBN 0–415–10238–3

Figures

Tables

Preface

The development of tourism studies as a legitimate area of academic study in the 1980s has been reflected in the growing literature appearing in specialist journals, the expanding range of textbooks and more specialist research monographs and edited books. As with any subject, its intellectual development is not simply measured in terms of the volume of material published. The effect of such literature on the way in which students and educators are encouraged to think about the subject and to pursue new avenues of research is one way of gauging the impact of such studies. The recent methodological and philosophical debates encapsulated in D.G. Pearce and R. Butler's (1993) *Tourism Research: Critiques and Challenges* highlight many of the problems associated with tourism research in the early 1990s, particularly the failure to link multidisciplinary research together to develop a more holistic understanding of tourism, tourists and their impact. This book is by no means a response to their call for a more explicit methodological concern in tourism research: it is an attempt to highlight how disciplinary research on tourism and transport can be integrated to provide a clearer understanding of the interface and relationship between tourism and transport. But why publish a book on the topic? Are there no equivalent studies which deal with the matter adequately? The simple answer is no. Despite the rapid expansion in tourism publishing in the 1980s, no book explicitly deals with the relationship between tourism and transport.

Existing studies aimed at BTEC national and higher national courses in the UK and general texts published in North America contain common elements concerned with tourism and transport and many of these books deal with the topic admirably in an empirical sense. Yet the relationship between tourism and transport is rarely discussed in the popular tourism textbooks. Such books do not consider what is meant by a tourist transport system and how the needs of the traveller are incorporated into management systems beyond a simplistic level. Even recognised undergraduate tourism textbooks pay very little attention to the tourism–transport interface. For this reason, an introductory text may help to stimulate some thought and discussion on the role of transport in tourism and vice versa. This book is also part of a new series – *Topics in Tourism* – aimed at both the BTEC and first year degree level student. The main aim of the series is to introduce and systematically discuss a range of concepts and ideas related to a theme, which are then developed through the use of supporting case studies. In this case, the book is also designed to be a starting point for those interested in research on transport studies and tourism, because the content and bibliography may serve as an introductory review for more advanced degree level students.

Academics write books for many different reasons. In this instance, the continual absence of any discussion of transport for tourism in the academic journals and textbooks which were either very rudimentary or highly specialised and technical prompted research on transport and tourism beyond the few paragraphs or chapters found in many of the established tourism textbooks.

This book is not intended to be a rewrite of the main themes discussed in existing textbooks. Instead it is a fresh look at what is sometimes construed as a mundane and specialist area of study dominated by a small number of tourism-related publications, prompting the reader to consider some of the relationships which exist in providing transport for tourists. As a short introductory book it does not claim to present a comprehensive review of the topic. It focuses on some of the key issues which transport providers, decision-makers, managers and tourists face in the use, operation and management of tourist transport. If the book raises the profile of transport issues in tourism and stimulates debate among its readers, reviewers and critics then it will have succeeded in establishing a consensus of opinion on tourist transport as a legitimate area of study that has hitherto remained the subject of highly specialised studies. Inevitably, some people will question some of the ideas raised in this book, but this can only assist in fostering more discussion of an area frequently overlooked in the tourism literature.

Inevitably, certain people have helped to shape the thoughts and ideas in this book. My thanks go to Chris Young, Christ Church College, Canterbury, who read the entire manuscript in his usual diligent and critical manner. I am also indebted to John Hills for drawing all the diagrams and also to Lisa who typed (and retyped) the manuscript with precision and speed. Other former colleagues such as Eric Laws and Nicola Clark at Christ Church College have debated issues discussed in the book, even though they may have felt the ideas were rather esoteric at times. No list of acknowledgements would be complete without a mention of the undergraduate Tourism Studies students at Christ Church College of Higher Education, Canterbury, who have acted as a springboard for some of the ideas developed in this book. I hope some of them actually read it! Francesca Weaver and Laura Large at Routledge have proved to be helpful and efficient in dealing with the book, while my wife, Sue, has been a constant source of encouragement, as ever. Lastly, I would like to acknowledge the continued fruitful debate which colleagues have engaged in when bouncing ideas around in seminars and over a cup of coffee.

Stephen Page

Acknowledgements

The author would like to thank the following for permission to use tables in the text: The Department of Statistics (New Zealand) for permission to reproduce Tables 2.1, 2.2 and 2.3; the British Tourist Authority for Tables 2.4 and 2.5 and Butterworth–Heinemann to reproduce Table 2.6 and for permission to quote from *Tourism Management*. I am also indebted to Prentice Hall for permission to reproduce Table 5.6 and D. Fulton publishers for Table 5.7. Belhaven granted permission to reproduce Table 6.1 and Town and County Planning kindly consented to the use of Table 6.6. I am also grateful to British Airways for the opportunity to reproduce Tables 6.2, 6.3 and 6.4 and to use material from their Environmental Report. John Wiley and Sons, the *Journal of Travel Research* and HMSO also kindly provided permission to quote from their publications. If any unknowing use has been made of copyright material, could owners please contact the author via the publishers as every effort has been made to trace owners and to obtain permission.

1
Introduction

Transport is acknowledged as one of the most significant factors which has contributed to the international development of tourism. According to Gayle and Goodrich (1993), in 1991 the international tourism industry employed 112 million people world-wide and generated over $2.5 trillion at 1989 prices. Furthermore, 443 million tourists travelled abroad in 1990, with internal tourist arrivals expected to rise by 4.2 per cent in the 1990s, generating a significant demand for tourist transport.

Transport is an integral part of tourism which facilitates the movement of holidaymakers, business travellers, those people visiting friends and relatives and undertaking educational and health tourism. Transport is also a key element of the 'tourist experience' (Pearce 1982) and some commentators (e.g. Middleton 1988; Tourism Society 1990) view it as an integral part of the tourism industry. Despite the controversy over the extent to which tourism can be defined as both an industry and a service activity, it is widely recognised that tourism combines a broad range of economic activities and services designed to meet the needs of tourists.

Transport provides the essential link between tourism origin and destination areas. Transport can also form the focal point for tourist activity in the case of cruising and holidays which contain a significant component of travel (e.g. coach holidays and scenic rail journeys). Here the mode of transport forms a context and controlled environment for tourists' movement between destinations and attractions, often through the medium of a 'tour'. The mode of transport tourists choose can often form an integral part of their journeys and experience, a feature often neglected in the existing research on tourism. So how has transport been viewed in existing textbooks on tourism?

Tourism studies and tourist transportation

The majority of influential tourism textbooks are a product of the 1980s and early 1990s, despite some notable exceptions (e.g. McIntosh 1973; Burkart and Medlik 1974, 1975). The rapid expansion in the number of tourism textbooks published is one indication of the emergence of the subject as a serious area of study at vocational, degree and postgraduate level throughout the world. As many national governments recognise the contribution tourism can make to GDP and national economic development, the expansion of their tourism industries has led to a consideration of the immediate and long-term human resource and training requirements. New courses have developed to fill a niche in the educational marketplace and these have generated a demand for course materials to meet the international expansion of tourism education (Goodenough and Page 1993). The range of available textbooks for tourism studies has generally been written from a North American (e.g. Lundberg 1980; Mathieson and Wall 1982; Mill and Morrison 1985; Murphy 1985; Gunn 1988; McIntosh and Goeldner 1990), European (e.g. Foster 1985; Lavery 1989; Laws 1991; Ryan 1991; Witt et al. 1991) or Australasian perspective (e.g. Pearce 1987, 1992; Collier 1989; Leiper 1990; Bull 1991; Hall 1991; Perkins and Cushman 1993), with few widely available student texts written from an Asian or Less Developed World perspective. An examination of these textbooks indicates that travel and transport is a topic frequently cited in relation to its role as a facilitator of the expansion of tourism, as new technology (e.g. the railway and jet engine) and novel forms of marketing and product developments (e.g. package holidays) have contributed to the development of tourism as a mass consumer product. For example, Hall (1991: 22) argues that 'the evolution of tourism in Australia is inseparable from the development of new forms of transport' and 'a clear relationship exists between transport development and tourism growth' (Hall 1991: 80). The development and expansion of tourist destinations are, in part, based on the need for adequate access to resort areas, their attractions and resources. Hence the relationship between transport and tourism is usually conceptualised in terms of accessibility within most tourism textbooks.

A number of other textbooks (e.g. Holloway 1989; Mill 1992) have sought to develop this relationship one stage further, by discussing the historical development of tourist travel and accessibility, and the principles governing tourism's expansion within the context of different forms of tourist transport (e.g. air, road, rail and sea travel). Yet tourism studies do not have a monopoly on the analysis of transportation for tourists. Textbooks on transport studies indirectly discuss the movement of tourists. Many transport studies texts are written from a disciplinary perspective such as economics (e.g. Stubbs et al. 1980; Glaister 1981; Bell et al. 1983; Banister and Button 1991) while other texts focus on the operational, organisational and management issues associated with different forms of transport (e.g. Button 1982, 1991; Faulks 1990). However, the 'tourist' is rarely mentioned in these books as the term 'passenger' is usually substituted. The difficulty here is that the term 'passenger' fails to distinguish between the reasons for tourist movement, inferring an impersonal contractual relationship where operators move people between areas on transport systems, systems which are only concerned with the throughput of passengers. In reality, a different situation exists, with transport operators in the 1990s equally concerned with many of the issues facing the tourism industry, particularly customer care and the tourist's experience while travelling. Owing to the choice of transport available and the competitive environment for tourist travel in free market economies, transport operators recognise the importance of ensuring that the travel experience is both pleasurable and fulfils consumers' expectations. In state-planned economies, both the demand and supply for tourist transport is regulated by the state and a different political and ideological agenda affects the availability of tourist transport compared with free market economies.

Halsall (1992) identifies the overlap between transport, tourism and recreation, arguing that in reality it is often difficult to distinguish between tourist and non-tourist use of different forms of transport: the exceptions are dedicated forms of tourist transport such as charter flights and cruises. Even so, operators such as British Railways (hereafter BR) do not use the term 'tourist', preferring to distinguish between 'business and leisure' travellers when identifying their potential passenger market. Therefore, the tourist is not explicitly recognised as such, but as a passenger. In contrast, some tourism researchers recognise the tourist trip as an important feature to examine in its own right (Pearce 1987; S.L.J. Smith 1989), although it receives only scant attention due to the simplistic notions of the tourism–transport relationship.

Consequently, the relationship between tourism and transport is rarely discussed in the context of the 'tourist experience'.

Both transport and tourism studies fail to provide an explicit and holistic framework in which to assess the transportation of tourists. For this reason, it is possible to build on the complementarity of these two areas of study to identify the concept of the 'tourist transportation system' which highlights the integral role of transport in the 'tourist experience'. This also has the potential to accommodate different approaches to the analysis of tourist travel and transportation. What is a 'tourist transport system'?

The tourist transport system: a framework for analysis

To understand the complexity and relationships which co-exist between tourism and transport, one needs to build a framework which can synthesise the different factors and processes affecting the organisation, operation and management of activities associated with tourist travel. The objective of such a framework is to provide a means of understanding how tourists interact with transport, the processes and factors involved and their effect on the travel component of the overall 'tourist experience'. Any such framework for analysing tourist transport needs to incorporate the tourist's use of transport services from the pre-travel booking stage through to the completion of the journey and which recognises the significance of the service component. It also needs to incorporate the different modes of transport used by tourists (e.g. air travel by scheduled or charter service, sea travel using ferries or cruise ships, and land-based transportation including car, rail, coach, motor caravan, motorbike and bicycle).

One methodology used by researchers to understand the nature of the tourism phenomenon is a systems approach (Laws 1991). The main purpose of such an approach is to rationalise and simplify the real world complexity of tourism into a number of constructs and components which highlight the inter-related nature of tourism. Since tourism studies are a multidisciplinary area of study (Gilbert 1990), a systems approach can accommodate a variety of different perspectives because it does not assume a predetermined view of tourism. Instead, it enables one to understand the broader issues and factors which affect tourism, together with the inter-relationships between different components in the system. According to Leiper (1990), a system can be defined as a set of elements or parts that are connected to each other by at least one

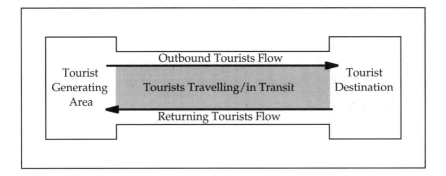

Figure 1.1 A tourism system

Source: After Simmons and Leiper (1993)

Notes: Input – tourist decision to travel and movement to destination
Output – tourist holiday experience
Flow – tourist travel

distinguishing principle. In this case, tourism is the distinguishing principle which connects the different components in the system around a common theme. Laws (1991: 7) developed this idea a stage further by providing a systems model of the tourism industry in which the key components were: the inputs, outputs and external factors conditioning the system (e.g. the external business environment, consumer preferences, political factors and economic issues). As external factors are important influences upon tourism systems, the system can be termed 'open', which means that it can easily be influenced by factors aside from the main 'inputs'. The links within the system can be examined in terms of 'flows' between components and these flows may highlight the existence of certain types of relationships between different components (Figure 1.1).

For example:

- What effect does an increase in the cost of travel have on the demand for travel?
- How does this have repercussions for other components in the system?
- Will it reduce the number of tourists travelling?

A systems approach has the advantage of allowing the researcher to consider the effect of such changes to the tourism system to assess the likely impact on other components.

Leiper (1990) identified the following elements of a tourism system: a tourist; a traveller-generating region; tourism destination regions; transit routes for tourists travelling between generating destination areas, and the travel and tourism industry (e.g. accommodation, transport, the firms and organisations supplying services and products to tourists). In this analysis, transport forms an integral part of the tourism system, connecting the tourist-generating and destination region, which is represented in terms of the volume of travel. The significance of transport in the tourism system is also apparent in the model developed by Laws (1991), where a series of smaller sub-systems was also identified (e.g. the transport system) which can be analysed as a discrete activity in its own right while also forming an integral part of the wider 'tourism system'. Thus, a 'tourist transport' system is a framework which embodies the entire tourist experience of travelling on a particular form of transport. The analytical value of such an approach is that it enables one to understand the overall process of tourist travel from both the supplier's and the purchaser's perspective while identifying the organisations which influence and regulate tourist transport. How does this book aim to integrate tourist travel more fully into the study of tourism?

Structure of the book

This book is not intended to be a comprehensive review of transport for tourism in view of the objectives of the new *Topics in Tourism* series. It is designed as a framework in which the reader can gain a clearer understanding of the tourist transport system and some of the ways in which we can analyse the provision, operation and factors influencing this activity. One objective of the chapters in this book is to overcome the existing perception of tourist transport as a passive element in the tourist's experience which has to be endured to reach a destination area (cruising and touring excepted). The actual process of travelling is an integral part of the tourist's experience even though it is perceived as less important than the activities and pursuits of tourists in the destination. The book offers a number of perspectives of tourist transport which the reader may find as a useful starting point for further research on transport and tourism. One underlying theme emphasised throughout the book is that transport for tourism constitutes a 'service' which is increasingly judged by consumers and providers in relation to the quality, standards and level of satisfaction it engenders. For this reason, both a systems approach and the emphasis on the multidisciplinarity of tourist transport help to transcend the rather fragmented view of this aspect of tourism studies.

In Chapter 2, the multidisciplinarity of tourist transport is examined, drawing upon the concepts and approaches used in economics, geography and marketing. Each area of study provides a useful insight into the specialised nature of research on tourism and transport studies which is rarely discussed in terms of the way each complements our understanding of the tourist transport system. As Leiper and Simmons show, researchers from different disciplines consider various aspects of tourism depending on their background and focus, which inevitably means that they consider specific inputs, outputs and external factors which affect the tourist transport system. For this reason, it is useful to examine some of the common approaches and concepts used by different disciplines in analysing tourist transport. Chapter 3 considers the role of transport policy and planning and its effect on operational and consumer issues, and the progress towards a common transport policy in the EC. A case study of tourist travel by rail in the UK is used to illustrate how national transport policy objectives are implemented and the significance for tourist experiences of rail service provision. This is followed in Chapter 4 with an analysis of the demand aspects of tourist travel and the data sources available to tourism researchers. Chapter 5 looks at the supply of tourist transport, focusing on the supply chain and how companies with transport interests seek to exercise control over the distribution and quality of tourist travel services. The response of the US domestic airline market to deregulation is used to illustrate how concentration in the aviation market has affected the supply of services. The human and environmental consequences of tourist travel and the operation of different modes of tourist transport are then discussed in Chapter 6, concluding with a discussion of the potential for developing sustainable tourist transport. Chapter 7 concludes the book, examining some of the main issues discussed in the book while identifying further directions for research on what is a rapidly changing area of study.

Questions

1 To what extent is tourist transport considered as an area of study in transport and tourism studies?
2 What is the value of a systems approach to the analysis of tourist transport?
3 What are the main features of a system?

Further reading

McIntosh, R. W. (1973) *Tourism: Principles and Philosophies*, Columbus, OH: Grid Inc.

This was the first tourism textbook to be published, and it is still a useful introduction to the subject. The concept of a tourism system is dealt with in:

Laws, E. (1991) *Tourism Marketing: Service Quality Management Perspectives*, Cheltenham: Stanley Thornes.
Leiper, N. (1990) *Tourism Systems: An Interdisciplinary Perspective*, Palmerston North: Massey University.
Wheatcroft, S. (1978) 'Transport, tourism and the service industry', *Chartered Institute of Transport Journal* 38, 7: 197–206.

2
Understanding tourist transport
Social science perspectives

Introduction

In the previous chapter, a systems approach introduced one way of understanding the complexity of tourist transport systems and the relationships between different components in such systems. Tourism, like transport studies, is a multidisciplinary field of study which has borrowed and refined concepts and theories from other social science subjects as it establishes itself as a legitimate area of academic study. This poses a number of problems for researchers when exploring the relationship between transport and tourism in the context of tourist transport systems. For example, what approaches and methods of study should one use to analyse tourist transport systems? In most cases, research is based on those social science disciplines with an interest in tourism and/or transport studies. This has an important bearing on the analysis of tourist transport systems because the type of questions a researcher asks, and the focus of their work, is often determined by their disciplinary background.

Each social science subject has its own range of concepts, research methods and literature and has made distinctive contributions to the study of tourism although no one discipline is all-embracing enough to understand the complexity of the tourist transport system (see *Annals of Tourism Research* special issue on 'Tourism: social science', 1991, for a more detailed discussion). For example, social science subjects such as social psychology, sociology, and business and management studies have an interest in tourism and transport studies although there is a relative paucity of published research which analyses the tourist transport system.

However, for the purpose of this book, there are three social science subjects which have made a direct contribution to the analysis of tourist transport systems. These are:

- Economics
- Geography
- Marketing

It must be stressed that because this is an introductory level book, it is only possible to outline some of the main principles which have been developed to analyse tourist transport. This chapter does not attempt to provide a comprehensive review of the literature and main areas of research on transport and tourism. A wide range of books has already been published in economics, geography and marketing which provide an insight into tourism and transport although none have developed a particular focus on transport for tourism. The approach adopted here is to use a number of case studies to illustrate the distinctive contribution which economists, geographers and marketers have made to the analysis of tourist transport, and readers are directed to the specialised studies in the text for a more detailed insight of particular issues.

The economist and tourist transport

The economist's approach to the analysis of tourist transport is based on two distinct areas of research, transport economics (e.g. Starkie 1976; Beesley 1989) and tourism economics (e.g. Bull 1991; Sinclair 1991), and each area of study uses similar concepts to understand how the tourist transport system functions. For this reason, it is useful to consider what issues are examined by economists as a basis for a more detailed discussion of the concepts they use.

What is economics?

Like many social science subjects, there is little agreement on how to define an area of study such as economics. However, according to Craven (1990: 3) 'economics is concerned with the economy or economic system . . . [and] . . . the problem of allocating resources is a central theme of economics, because most resources are scarce'.

Therefore Craven (1990: 4) argues that economics is the study of methods of allocating scarce resources and distributing the product of those resources, and the study of the consequences of these methods of allocation and distribution.

What is meant by scarcity and resources? The term scarcity is used to illustrate the fact that most resources in society are finite and decisions have to be made on the best way to use and sustain these resources. Economists define resources in terms of:

* natural resources (e.g. the land)
* labour (e.g. human resources and entrepreneurship)
* capital (e.g. man-made aids to assist in producing goods)

and collectively these resources constitute *the factors of production* which are used to produce commodities. These commodities can be divided into:

* goods (e.g. tangible products such as an aircraft)
* services (e.g. intangible items such as in-flight service – see Laws and Ryan 1992)

and the total output of all commodities in a country over a period of time, normally a year, is known as the *national product*. The creation of products and services is termed *production* and the use of these goods and services is called *consumption*. Since, in any society, the production of goods and services can only satisfy a small fraction of consumers' needs, choices have to be made on the allocation of resources to determine which goods and services to produce (Lipsey 1989). The way in which goods and services are divided among people has been examined by economists in terms of the distribution of income and the degree of equality and efficiency in their distribution. Many of these issues are dealt with under the heading of 'microeconomics' which Craven succinctly defines as:

> . . . the study of individual decisions and the interactions of these decisions . . . [including] . . . consumers' decisions on what to buy, firms' decisions on what to produce and the interactions of these decisions, which determine whether people can buy what they would like, whether firms can sell all that they produce and the profits firms make by providing and selling.
>
> (Craven 1990: 4)

Therefore, microeconomics is concerned with certain issues, namely:

- the firm
- the consumer
- production and selling
- the demand for goods
- the supply of goods

Economists also examine a broader range of economic issues in terms of *macroeconomics* which is concerned with

> the entire economy and interactions within it, including the population, income, total unemployment, the average rate of price increases (the inflation rate), the extent of companies' capacities to produce goods and the total amount of money in use in the country.
> (Craven 1990: 5)

Therefore, macroeconomics is mainly concerned with:

- how the national economy operates
- employment and unemployment
- inflation
- national production and consumption
- the money supply in a country

Within micro- and macroeconomics, both transport and tourism economists examine different aspects of the tourist transport system which is based on the analysis of the concepts of demand and supply.

Demand

Within economics, the concern with the allocation of resources to satisfy individuals' desire to travel means that transport economists examine the *demand* for different modes of travel and the competition between such modes in relation to price, speed, convenience and reliability. Economists attempt to understand what affects people's travel behaviour and the significance of transport as something which is rarely consumed for its own sake: it is usually demanded as a means of consuming some other goods or service (i.e. commuting to work or the travel component of a holiday). The demand for tourist transport is also characterised (Mill 1992: 83–4) by:

- its almost instantaneous and unpredictable nature, which requires operators to build overcapacity in the supply to avoid dissatisfied travellers

- the variability in demand, ranging from *derived demand* (where tourist transport is a facilitating mechanism to achieve another objective, such as business travel) to *primary demand* which is the pursuit of travel for vacation purposes
- non-priced items (e.g. service quality, reliability and punctuality).

Transport economists have developed mathematical models to analyse the trip-making behaviour of travellers (Ortuzar and Willumsen 1990), the factors influencing demand and why variations occur in the trip-making behaviour of consumers due to relationships between socio-economic factors (e.g. age, income, profession and family status) and the effect of macroeconomic conditions (e.g. the state of the economy). In contrast tourism economists have examined the demand for travel and tourist products, recognising the significance of demand as a driving force in the economy. This stimulates entrepreneurial activity to produce the goods and services to satisfy the demand (Bull 1991). More specifically, tourism economists examine the *effective demand* for goods or services which is the aggregate or overall demand over a period of time. Since income has an important effect on tourism demand, economists measure the impact using a term known as the *elasticity of demand*. As Bull (1991: 37) has shown, it is measured using a ratio calculated thus:

$$\text{Elasticity of demand} = \frac{\text{percentage change in tourism demand}}{\text{percentage change in disposable income}}$$

in relation to two equal time periods. The significance of this concept is that the demand for goods to fulfil basic needs (e.g. food, water and shelter) is relatively unchanging or *inelastic* while the demand for luxury items, such as holiday and pleasure travel, is variable or *elastic*, being subject to fluctuations in demand due to factors such as income or price. Thus, elasticity is used to express the extent to which tourists are sensitive to changes in price and service. For example, primary demand is usually more elastic than derived demand. In tourist transportation, researchers recognise the importance of price which is acknowledged as a more complex issue than income, owing to the varying impact of exchange rates, the relative prices of destinations and the high level of competition between destinations for tourists. Furthermore, the different elements which comprise the tourism product (e.g. transport, accommodation and attractions) are complementary and it is difficult to separate out one individual item as exerting a dominant effect on price since each is inter-related in terms of what is purchased and consumed.

To assess the impact of price on the demand for tourism, economists examine the *price elasticity of demand*, where an inverse relationship exists between demand and price (Bull 1991). For example, it is generally accepted that the greater the price, the less demand there will be for a tourism product owing to the limited amount of the population's disposable income which is available to purchase the product which is calculated thus:

Price elasticity of demand =

$$\frac{\text{percentage change in quantity of tourism product demanded}}{\text{percentage change in tourism product price}}$$

Other contributory factors which influence the demand for tourism include the impact of tourist taxation, the amount of holiday entitlement available to potential tourists as well as the effects of weather, climate and cultural preferences for holidaymaking which are expressed in terms of seasonality. These factors also need to be viewed in the context of the economics of operating each mode of tourist transport to understand how the demand is met by the operators' supply of a service. However, in view of the variations that exist between different forms of demand for modes of transport, readers should consult more detailed studies on the economics of transport (e.g. Bell *et al.* 1983; Button 1982; Glaister 1981; and Stubbs *et al.* 1980). The significance of tourist demand for transport is examined in case study 1. This considers how tourism demand for a country relatively inaccessible and distant from many of the world's main tourist-generating markets has realised its potential in the late 1970s, 1980s and 1990s as additional capacity for tourist transport was provided. Hence the case study also suggests that the demand for tourist transport cannot be examined in isolation from supply issues, which are introduced in the next section, after the case study.

Case study 1: The demand for international tourist travel to New Zealand

Tourism was one of New Zealand's fastest growing economic activities in the 1980s and early 1990s, generating NZ $4,251 million in 1990. New Zealand has built an enviable international image as a tourist destination with its National Park system comprising 8 per cent of the land area. It also has an abundance of underdeveloped areas and open spaces, urban heritage and cultural resources (Page 1993a) which are very appealing to international visitors (Pearce 1992). New Zealand has managed to market its natural resources and scenic landscape, which covers 267,000 km², to visitors. It has a variety of landscape types: from sub-tropical through the thermal and volcanic central area of the North Island to the alpine and fiord landscape of the South Island (Page 1989a). Although New Zealand is relatively distant from many of the world's main tourism markets (North America and Western Europe – see Table 2.1) its location in the East Asia and South Pacific region has meant that it has benefited from a growth in tourism markets in Japan, Taiwan and other South East Asian newly industrialised countries. New Zealand is a long-haul destination, implying that journey times are in excess of 4 hours' flying time, often in the 10–12 hour time band

Table 2.1 Distances from Auckland airport to selected overseas destinations

Destination	Distance (km)*
Adelaide	3,247
Brisbane	2,293
Hong Kong	9,145
Honolulu	7,086
Los Angeles	10,480
Melbourne	2,635
Perth	5,400
Rarotonga	3,013
San Francisco	10,503
Singapore	8,410
Sydney	2,158
Tokyo	8,837

* These are airport-to-airport great circle distances.
Source: Department of Statistics (1992: 36).

Case study 1 (*continued*)

(the exception being Tonga and Australia – see Table 2.1). Nevertheless, New Zealand's distance from other countries has meant it places a heavy reliance on air travel to encourage an expansion in tourist arrivals.

The growth in international tourist arrivals

One theme which is of interest to tourism economists is the evolution of tourism demand in particular countries and the factors which explain why certain trends emerged. In New Zealand, international tourist arrivals expanded from 2,803 in 1945 to 967,062 in 1991 (Figure 2.1). As Figure 2.1 shows, international arrivals expanded rapidly in the 1950s, at an average rate of 9.5 per cent per annum. In the 1960s, arrivals expanded at a higher rate, averaging a growth of 15.6 per cent per annum. The 1970s saw a slow-down in growth to an average growth rate of 10.7 per cent, with the oil crisis reducing demand as air fares were forced to rise. This was replaced by a significant growth in tourist arrivals, which increased by 7.55 per cent in 1980–8, but by 26.7 per cent between 1988 and 1991 as the number of visitors rose to just under a million (Table 2.2). Given the reliance on air transport, some of the growth in the late 1960s can be attributed to the introduction of larger commercial aircraft (e.g. the McDonnell Douglas DC 10 and Boeing 747) which increased the capacity on routes to/from New Zealand and encouraged more cost-effective air travel. In the late 1980s, the introduction of the extended range Boeing 747–400 removed the need for refuelling stops on the New Zealand–Los Angeles arm of New Zealand–UK flights. New technology has not only reduced the flying time to New Zealand for long-haul markets but also led to greater fuel economies, reflected in more competitive fares. After 1980 the New Zealand government also licensed more carriers to fly into the country which greatly improved capacity (Table 2.3), as major airlines recognised the country's rising importance as a tourist destination. Although various factors have been cited to explain the expansion of international tourist arrivals in New Zealand, research by Hamilton (1988) noted that

Case study 1 (*continued*)

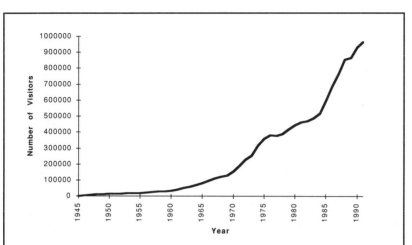

Figure 2.1 International tourist arrivals in New Zealand, 1945–92
Source: New Zealand Tourist and Publicity Department/Department of Statistics.

Table 2.2 Source areas for international arrivals in New Zealand, 1990 and 1991

Country	1990	1991
Australia	327,459	343,299
United States	136,946	139,030
Japan	100,348	105,716
United Kingdom	78,528	87,963
Canada	32,268	33,545
Germany	24,865	32,171
Singapore	14,767	15,251
Taiwan	14,939	11,049
Hong Kong	16,092	16,114
Sweden	8,333	8,288
Malaysia	7,953	9,783
Switzerland	9,916	11,298
Netherlands	7,292	7,624
Fiji	7,466	7,512
Indonesia	4,290	4,898
France	3,906	3,829
Tahiti (French Polynesia)	3,773	3,997
Papua New Guinea	2,641	2,853
South Africa	1,767	1,967

Source: Department of Statistics (1992: 217).

Table 2.3 New Zealand airline operations – date of commencement and routes operated (excluding Air New Zealand)

Date	Airline	Routes now operated
10 Jul 1949	Canadian Airlines International	Toronto/Vancouver/Honolulu/Auckland* Toronto/Vancouver/Honolulu/Nadi/Auckland
01 Apr 1961	Qantas	Sydney/Melbourne/Brisbane/Perth/Adelaide/Hobart/Cairns/Auckland/Christchurch/ Wellington Sydney/Auckland/Honolulu/Los Angeles Melbourne/Auckland/Papeete/Los Angeles Auckland/Norfolk Island
04 Apr 1963	British Airways	London/Bangkok/Kuala Lumpur/Melbourne/Auckland London/Singapore/Perth/Auckland
02 Dec 1965	UTA	Noumea/Auckland/Papeete
01 Oct 1974	Air Pacific	Nadi/Auckland
31 May 1976	Singapore Airlines	Singapore/Auckland Singapore/Sydney/Melbourne/Auckland (freight)
25 Feb 1978	Polynesian Airlines	Apia/Tonga/Auckland Apia/Tonga/Auckland/Sydney
01 May 1979	Continental Airlines	Los Angeles/Honolulu/Auckland/Sydney/Melbourne/Brisbane
01 Dec 1979	Air Nauru	Nauri/Auckland
01 Jul 1980	Japan Airlines	Tokyo/Auckland Tokyo/Christchurch/Auckland Nagoya/Auckland

Table 2.3 *Continued*

Date	Airline	Routes now operated
03 Dec 1985	Cathay Pacific	Hong Kong/Auckland
20 Dec 1985	Aerolineas Argentinas	Buenos Aires/Auckland/Sydney
11 Feb 1986	United Airlines	San Francisco/Honolulu/Auckland/Sydney/Brisbane
08 Nov 1987	Air Caledonie	Noumea/Auckland
05 Dec 1987	Thai Airways	Bangkok/Auckland
04 Nov 1988	Garuda Indonesia	Jakarta/Denpasar/Bali/Auckland
01 Nov 1989	Air Vanuatu	Port Vila/Auckland
05 Dec 1989	Malaysia Airlines	Kuala Lumpur/Brisbane/Auckland
21 Feb 1990	American Airlines	Honolulu/Auckland*
13 Jun 1990	Solomon Airlines	Honiara/Port Vila/Auckland Honiara/Port Vila/Nadi/Auckland
16 Jul 1990	Niue Airlines	Niue/Auckland
01 May 1991	Southern World Airlines	Los Angeles/Honolulu/Auckland/Melbourne
01 Jul 1991	Royal Tongan Airlines	Tonga/Auckland

Note: * Code – shared services.

Source: Department of Statistics (1992: 35).

Case study 1 (*continued*)

in the late 1980s it exceeded world-wide rates of growth for tourist trips and nights spent overseas. To understand the detailed reasons for this growth would require a major investigation of the different source areas for international arrivals (see Table 2.2) and why they chose to visit the country. For example, in-house research by the former New Zealand Tourist and Publicity Department (see Pearce 1992 for changes to the organisation of public sector management of tourism in New Zealand) considered the elasticity of demand in different international market segments to understand how they were performing as source areas.

Research by Henshall *et al.* (1985) examined the tourists' decision to visit New Zealand as part of a fly–drive package and observed the significance of promotional campaigns and marketing. Therefore any detailed analysis of these trends in arrivals will certainly need to consider how New Zealand's improved accessibility and geographical characteristics are being positively marketed to visitors to encourage an expansion in visitors (Pearce 1992). But the expansion of tourist arrivals may have important social, cultural, environmental and economic effects for New Zealand. Recent forecasts of visitor arrivals by the New Zealand Tourism Department are optimistic that by the year 2000, with positive promotion, arrivals will reach 3 million. Yet for New Zealand to achieve 3 million arrivals, an adequate *supply* of tourist transport and supporting infrastructure needs to be provided.

Supply

Economists are also interested in the *supply* of a commodity (e.g. tourist transport) which is often seen as a function of its price and the price of alternative goods. Price is often influenced by the cost of the factors of production, but in the case of tourist transport, it is difficult to identify the real cost of travel. For example, state subsidies for rail travel in Europe are used to support the supply of services in the absence of a major demand for social reasons (Whitelegg 1987). The price charged may not always reflect the true cost due to subsidies, particularly where tourist transport providers use cross-subsidies in their operations. Cross-subsidisation implies that profits from more lucrative routes are used to support uneconomic and unviable services to maintain a route network, thereby increasing the choice of destinations. According to Bull (1991: 78), the supply of tourist transport can be characterised by:

- major capital requirements for passenger carriage (e.g. the cost of aircraft, passenger trains and ferries)
- government regulations and restrictions to monitor the supply which is determined by state policy
- competitive reaction from other businesses involved in tourist transportation
- a high level of expertise required to operate and manage tourist transport enterprises.

Bull (1991) suggests that the principal questions which economists are interested in from the supply side are:

- What to produce.
- How to produce it.
- When and where to produce it.

From the transport operator's perspective, the main objective in supply terms is to maximise profitability from the available capacity which is usually expressed in terms of the *load factor*. Transport companies can maximise passenger revenue by minimising costs and pricing their product or service at a competitive rate. Certain travel markets are very price sensitive, which means that consumers may be easily persuaded to switch to another operator or mode of transport if the price rises beyond a critical level (the demand for youth travel on express coach services is a good example of a price-sensitive market). Despite price sensitivity, airlines and other modes of transport distinguish between scheduled routes which operate a regular timetabled service and charge higher fares and charter services operated on behalf of tour operators to carry holidaymakers who have purchased a transport-only component or package holiday from the tour operator. The price differential for scheduled and charter passengers is reflected in the passenger load factor which the scheduled airline needs to reach to achieve a profit (see the case study of Singapore International Airlines in Chapter 5). Scheduled routes charge a higher tariff but operate on a lower load factor compared with charter flights where a lower unit cost is charged but a higher load factor (often 90 per cent) is needed to yield a profit. Seasonality in the demand for tourist transport services may affect the load factor and peak usage at popular times means that transport operators use premium pricing to manage the supply and maximise profit to offset losses in times of limited demand.

Economists also have an interest in macroeconomic issues associated with the supply of tourist transport services and the structure of the market system in which companies operate. For example, economists have examined the effect of company strategy in the tourism and transport sectors in response to market competition which may affect the management, operation and provision of services to consumers. These different market conditions may range from near perfect competition to a situation where the three following conditions may occur:

oligopoly – which is a situation where the control of the supply of a
   service is by a small number of suppliers;
monopoly – where exclusive control of services is by a single supplier
duopoly – where two companies control the supply of services.
(See Bull 1991: 60–5 for a more detailed discussion.)

For the consumer, such activities may have a significant effect on the choice, price and degree of competition which occurs. In some cases, a monopoly situation or a variant may lead to anti-competitive practices and may not necessarily be in the public's interest, although arguments contrary to this view have also been expressed in relation to the break up of BR's provision of rail services in the UK (see Chapter 3). Transport and tourism economists have also retained an interest in the macroeconomic effects of tourist transport on national economies. Tourist use of transport is a major contributor to the balance of payments when examining the economic benefits of tourism. Such considerations have an important bearing on public or private sector investment decisions when examining the costs and benefits of building new tourist transport infrastructure (e.g. the construction of a new airport). Issues related to the employment-generating potential of new tourist transport infrastructure and the effect on income generation for local economies feature prominently in these investment decisions. Economists also use complex research techniques such as multiplier analysis (see Archer 1989) to evaluate the secondary or indirect economic benefits of additional tourist expenditure for local areas. There is also a growing awareness among economists of the environmental costs of tourist transport (Banister and Button 1992).

Geography and tourist transport

Within geography, the study of tourist transport has largely been undertaken by transport geographers (see Knowles 1993 for an excellent review of recent studies in transport geography) and tourism geographers (Pearce 1987, 1990). The concepts developed by transport geographers to study the relationships, interactions and locational aspects of transport systems have been directly applied to tourism geography (see Pearce 1990). The main concern of geographers when considering tourist transport can be related to three key concepts which characterise the study of geography:

- space – area, usually the earth's surface
- location – the position of something within space
- place – an identifiable position on the earth's surface.

Therefore, geographers are interested in the spatial expression of tourist transport as a vital link between tourist-generating and tourist-receiving areas. In particular, geographers are concerned with the patterns of human activity associated with tourist travel and how different processes lead to the formation of geographical patterns of tourist travel at different scales, ranging from the world to the national (e.g. country), regional (e.g. county) and local levels (e.g. an individual place). Previous geographical research on transport has looked at its role in different regions, its impact on economic development in terms of accessibility, the effect on the environment and the role of policy-making (see Farrington 1985). In many of the popular transport geography textbooks (e.g. Hay 1973; Lowe and Moryadas 1975; Adams 1981; White and Senior 1983; Barke 1986; Hoyle and Knowles 1992) there are a number of fundamental concepts which geographers use to analyse the spatial components of transport. Geographers have typically analysed travel as a response to satisfy a human desire for movement and the spatial outcome of such journeys. They have also considered the spatial variables in the transport system (e.g. location and places) and how these affect the costs and production of other social and economic activities. For the geographer, transport facilitates the process of movement which has economic and budgetary costs while behavioural factors (e.g. perception and preferences for particular forms of transport) determine the journey in terms of the available infrastructure and routes. In analysing the transport system, geographers have considered:

- the linkages and flows within a transport system

- the location and places connected by these linkages (usually referred to as 'centres' and 'nodes')
- the system of catchments and relationships between places within the network.

(Modified from Taafe and Ganthier 1973.)

The following case study illustrates how geographers have applied these concepts to the analysis of tourist transport systems.

Case study 2: The geography of tourist transport in Ireland: air travel

Recent research by Horner (1991) on airport and air-route devel-opment in Ireland illustrates how the geographer can analyse tourist transport provision. Ireland is often perceived as peripheral to many of Europe's main international tourism markets, and air traffic is the dominant form of transport used by inbound and outbound tourists (see Page 1993b for a more detailed discussion of peripherality and tourist travel in Ireland). As Figure 2.2 shows, the main air routes and the amount of traffic carried on the routes is represented as a flow line. Each *flow* is between a series origins (e.g. Ireland) and destinations. The origin points or *nodes* are the airports from which visitors arrive and depart. For Ireland, the main flows are between:

- Dublin/London and mainland Europe
- Belfast/Belfast City and London
- Ireland and other places in England, Wales and Scotland.

These airports are the main entry and exit points for tourists using air transport and are called *gateways* (see Pearce 1987). From Figure 2.2 it is also possible to examine how the nodes are related to the catchment areas the airports serve, the type and frequency of services offered and the degree of spatial organisation. Figure 2.3 shows that between 1975 and 1990 there have been changes in the degree of accessibility provided by the growth in smaller regional airports in Ireland. In 1990, most areas within Ireland were within a 1-hour drive of an airport which gives rise to a distinct pattern of airport provision. The geographer analyses this

Case study 2 (*continued*)

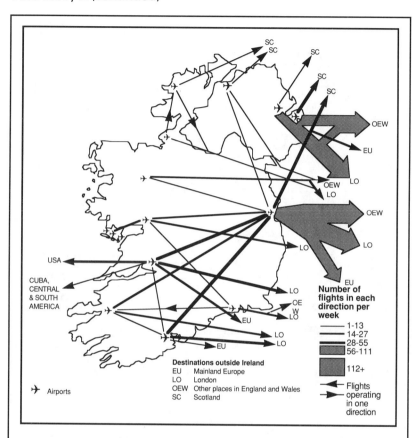

Figure 2.2 Air transport in Ireland

Source: After Horner (1991), using data for Summer 1990.

pattern in terms of the spatial hierarchy which exists in this pattern of provision by looking at the number and type of scheduled flights operated. Horner (1991) provided a ranking based on these two features to identify a hierarchy of airports which was a function of their airstrip size. The hierarchy comprised (Horner 1991):

Case study 2 (*continued*)

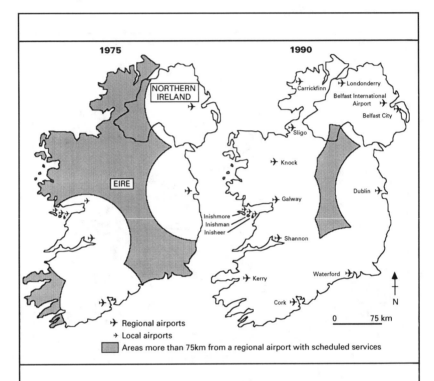

Figure 2.3 Changes in access to air travel in Ireland, 1975–90
Source: After Horner (1991).

I   Major airports capable of handling all sizes of aircraft (Belfast International, Dublin and Shannon), including 747 Jumbo jets.

IIa   Airports able to accommodate medium-sized jets operating scheduled services (e.g. Cork, Belfast City and Knock).

IIb   Similar airports without scheduled services (Baldonnel).

III   Airports with scheduled services capable of accommodating small jets (Carrickfin, Co. Galway, Farranfare, Co. Kerry, Waterford, Co. Sligo).

IV   Other airstrips with shorter, hard-surface landing facilities.

V   Other landing areas, mainly grass.

Case study 2 (*continued*)

The hierarchy of airports provides scheduled services, and the linkages and flows between the airports indicate which routes passengers
use between the major gateways and smaller regional airports. This
leads to a pattern of 'hubs' (gateways) and 'spokes' (smaller airports)
and a distinctive spatial network. Geographers have developed
methods of assessing how different nodes are connected within the
network (e.g. the degree of connectivity) and how accessible different
nodes are within the network (see Lowe and Moryadas 1975 for a
more technical discussion). In the case of Ireland, the dominant
feature is the limited amount of north–south cross-border traffic in the
network. The significance of Great Britain/mainland Europe as
origins and destinations for much of the traffic is based on a small
number of hubs in Ireland. Aside from Dublin and Belfast, Shannon
is an important node, since it is 'a mandatory stopping place for
scheduled transatlantic flights originating or terminating in the
Republic of Ireland' (Horner 1991: 43).

Transport geographers are also interested in the air transport network
in Ireland in terms of how it evolved, the spatial processes which shaped
the development of the network and how geographical models and
theories might be used to examine the flows and interactions in the
network. Clearly, the role of government policy in shaping and regulating the network would also be of significance and this point is developed
further in Chapter 3. How have these concepts been used by tourism
geographers researching tourist use of transport?

Tourism geography and tourist transport

According to Pearce (1979), geographical research on tourism initially
focused on:

- the spatial analysis of the supply and demand for tourism
- the geography of tourist resorts
- tourist movements and flows
- the analysis of the impact of tourism
- the development of models of tourist space to understand the evolution and expression of tourism in specific locations.

Since the 1970s, tourism research has examined the patterns and processes associated with the development of international and domestic tourism. One particular skill which the geographer has contributed to the study of tourism is the ability to synthesise (i.e. sift, search and make sense of) the approaches and analysis of the tourism phenomenon undertaken by other disciplines. During the 1980s geographical research on tourism moved more from a traditional concern with regional case studies and descriptions of tourism in particular locations to a more systematic and analytical approach. This is reflected in the recognition of how a spatial perspective can contribute to the analysis of tourism. How have geographers viewed tourist transport?

According to Mansfeld (1992: 58) 'the use of various modes of transport in getting to the destination has several spatial consequences' associated with the distance travelled, amount of time involved in travelling and the mode of transport used.

Pearce (1990: 28) acknowledges that advances in transport technology have altered the patterns of tourist flows and made tourist travel more flexible and diffuse. Prior to the expansion of car ownership and mass air travel, the patterns of tourist travel were linear. It was constrained and confined to transport corridors (e.g. river and railway lines) or the destinations served by sea. Both air transport and car travel have provided new opportunities for more flexible patterns of travel, though, as Sealy (1992) suggests, air travel and the expansion of international tourism is largely a nodal transport system dependent upon the airports (the nodes) and the flights (the flows) serving them. In the case of the Mediterranean, Pearce (1987) indicates that the expansion of charter airlines has provided a closer link between the tourism markets and potential destinations, and the increase in the geographical range of charter aircraft (i.e. increased flying time) and reduced costs of air travel have led to an expansion in the scale and distribution of tourism in the Mediterranean.

One further concept which tourism geographers have examined is the patterns of tourist transport – namely the tour. A tour is a tourist-oriented form of travel and Pearce (1987) examines the patterns and flows of tourist traffic in terms of preferred routes of travel. In the case of New Zealand, Forer and Pearce (1984) examine the tour itineraries of coach operators to provide information on the patterns of travel and circuits of coach tours. They found that on the North Island of New Zealand, a series of linear tours existed between the major gateways – Auckland and Wellington – with tourists visiting popular resorts and attractions en route. On the South Island, a more complex series of looped tours existed. Many of these often originated and ended at Christchurch (the second largest gateway) as tourists explored the diverse range of landscapes and scenic locations associated with National Parks such as Mount Cook, Westland and Fiordland. Pearce and Elliot (1983) developed a statistical technique – the Trip Index – to examine the extent to which places visited by tourists were major destinations or just a stopover. The Trip Index was calculated thus:

$$\text{Trip Index} = \frac{\text{nights spent at the destination}}{\text{total number of nights spent on the trip}} \times 100$$

A Trip Index of 100 means that the entire trip was spent at one destination and a value of zero would mean that no overnight stay was made on the entire journey. Other features which the tourism geographer has examined in terms of tourist transport include the use of the private car and public transport (Halsall 1992). Pearce (1990) also notes the importance of transit services from airports to city centres, as well as tourist use of transport to tour sites in major cities such as the London underground system. In fact, the Docklands Light Railway which connects central London to London Docklands has also become a popular form of tourist transport in its own right (Page 1989b, c, 1993c). Thus, geographers have undertaken research on tourist transport systems at different spatial scales in 'terms of mode, routes and types of operation (e.g. scheduled/non-scheduled)' (Pearce 1990: 29) and the spatial patterns, processes and networks which facilitate tourist travel, thereby making destinations more accessible.

Marketing and tourist transport

When one considers the contribution of economics and geography to the analysis of tourist transport, it is evident that a wide range of research papers and books exist. In the case of marketing, the number of studies focused on tourist transport is limited because there is a tendency for marketing to be more visible and results oriented rather than based on the academic analysis of good practice. Promotional material and advertising campaigns constitute a major investment in time, money and creative thinking, with companies reluctant to highlight good practice which might undermine their future business potential. To understand how marketing is integral to the analysis of tourist transport, it is useful to examine the nature, organisation and activities undertaken by marketers. For this reason, it is pertinent to examine the principles used in marketing which can be applied to the analysis of tourist transport.

What is marketing?

According to Kotler and Armstrong (1991), marketing is a process whereby individuals and groups obtain the type of products or goods they value. These goods are created and exchanged through a social and managerial process which requires a detailed understanding of consumers and their wants and desires so that the product or service is effectively and efficiently delivered to the client or purchaser. Within tourism studies, there has been a growing interest in marketing (e.g. Middleton 1988; Jefferson and Lickorish 1988; Laws 1991) compared with transport studies which has tended to employ marketers when required to deal with such issues. In transport studies, marketing has assumed less importance than operational and organisational issues. Gilbert (1989) considers the growth and establishment of marketing within tourism and the critical role of a consumer orientation among transport providers. For example, British Airways explained its financial turnaround from a loss of £544 million in 1981/2 to a profit of £272 million in 1983/4 in terms of a greater marketing orientation based on recognising customer needs and setting about satisfying them (Gilbert 1989). In this respect, marketing has a fundamental role to play in analysing tourist transport. Within marketing, three key areas exist:

- strategic planning
- marketing research
- the marketing mix

Strategic planning

Within any business or company, there is a need to provide some degree of order or structure to its activities and to think ahead. This is essential if companies are to be able to respond to the competitive business environment in which organisations operate. For this reason, a formal planning process is necessary which is known as *strategic planning*. According to Kotler and Armstrong (1991: 29), strategic planning can be defined as 'the process of developing and maintaining a strategic fit between the organisation's goals and capabilities and its changing marketing opportunities'.

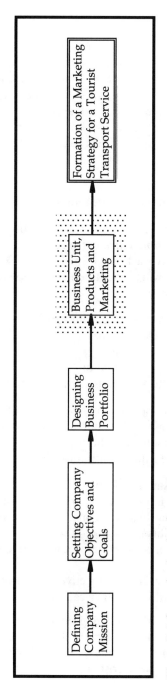

Figure 2.4 Strategic planning for tourist transport
Source: After Kotler and Armstrong (1991).

Businesses need to be aware of their position in the wider business environment and how they will respond to competition and new business opportunities within an organised framework. To illustrate how strategic planning operates and its significance to tourist transport, it is useful to focus on the structured approach devised by Kotler and Armstrong (1991). As Figure 2.4 shows, the first stage is the definition of an organisation's purpose which requires a company to consider:

- What business is it in?
- Who are its customers?
- What services do its customers require?

Following the definition of purpose, a company may incorporate these principles into a *mission statement* (see David 1989). This provides a focus for the company's activities which can be seen in the case of BR's Passenger's Charter which identified the following aims as part of its mission for customer service:

- A safe, punctual and reliable train service.
- Clean stations and clean trains.
- Friendly and efficient service.
- Clear and up to date information.
- A fair and satisfactory response if things go wrong.

Although a mission statement may be used for public relations purposes, as in the case of BR, one has to set objectives and goals. For example, the BR Passenger's Charter (which is discussed in more detail in Chapter 3) required the organisation to consider:

- What were its business objectives?
- Was it seeking to improve the market share of tourist travel by rail?
- Was the overriding business concern to improve the financial turnover and profitability?
- If so, what marketing objectives would need to be set to achieve these goals?
- Was the overall marketing objective to improve the public image of BR and to emphasise customer care and service standards?

Within this context, BR had to prepare a marketing strategy which acknowledged its business and marketing objectives and identified the resource requirements to achieve internal targets (e.g. achieving a greater market share of tourist travel) as well as the implications for research, sales and promotion and how this translates into an overall benefit for BR in a given timescale, such as a 1 or a 5 year period.

Obviously, the Passenger's Charter was only one aspect of strategic planning for BR's passenger services in 1992, but it does emphasise how important marketing and strategic planning are in launching such a new business initiative. The next stage following the setting of objectives and goals is termed the *business portfolio*. Here the company analyses its own products or services in terms of its own business expertise and how competitors' products and services may affect them. This is frequently undertaken as a SWOT analysis, which considers:

- the **S**trengths
- the **W**eaknesses
- the **O**pportunities
- the **T**hreats

of its products and services in the business environment. Case study 3 provides such an analysis for cross-Channel tourist transport services and shows how a company may need to respond to the competition and customers' needs, by finding ways of satisfying their needs through services which serve a niche or gap in the market.

Case study 3: Marketing cross-Channel tourist travel services

The opening of the Channel Tunnel will pose a major threat to the short-sea sector of the UK's cross-Channel ferry market (e.g. tourist movements between the ports of Dover, Folkestone, Ramsgate, Calais, Boulogne and Dunkerque) (see Figure 2.5). Despite the tunnel's high fixed capital cost, at over £10 billion, it will have relatively low operating costs compared with the ferry companies. Research has been undertaken on the potential impact of the opening and operation of the Fixed Link on the cross-Channel passenger market and has focused on the role of pricing a new tourist transport product/service which will provide competition for existing ferry operators (Page 1992a). Economists have also made forecasts of the potential impact of this development for prices and profitability of cross-Channel services with the advent of a new operator – Eurotunnel (Holliday *et al.* 1991).

Case study 3 (*continued*)

Since the tunnel will inevitably provide more competition for
existing tourist transport operators, it is interesting to examine
their strategic response to the tunnel which requires one to understand the scale of the challenge.

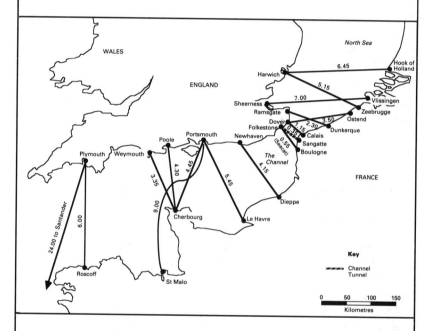

Figure 2.5 The cross-Channel ferry market

Although there is a great deal of uncertainty associated with the
potential impact of the tunnel, Eurotunnel's forecasters suggested
that approximately 14.6 million passengers would use the shuttle
service between the UK and France and 14 million would travel on
through train services between London–Paris–Brussels. This could
lead to a potential loss of up to 50 per cent of the ferry operators'

Case study 3 (*continued*)

passenger business, and a British Transport Authority (BTA) '1993 Cross-Channel Marketing Strategy' provided a strategic overview of the action which cross-Channel tourist transport operators (e.g. ferry companies, airlines, BR and Eurotunnel) would need to take to maximise the opportunities for inbound tourism to the UK. The report is useful in that it provides a SWOT analysis for each of the cross-Channel transport operators.

As Table 2.4 shows, the cross-Channel ferry operators have a number of issues which need to be addressed if they are to retain a significant market share of the future tourist traffic. Table 2.5 also outlines a similar analysis for the Eurotunnel shuttle service. One additional weakness which the BTA did not acknowledge in their study was the significance of public perception and limited knowledge of Eurotunnel's service in the months preceding the tunnel's opening. In January 1993, the Automobile Association undertook a survey of 522 car users in the UK to assess their perceptions of the tunnel. Although only 38 per cent had travelled abroad with a car in the past 3 years:

- nearly a third were unaware of how the shuttle service would operate and 19 per cent thought that you could drive a car through the tunnel!
- 50 per cent of those who had recently travelled abroad with a car stated that they would *not* use the tunnel
- two-thirds of those who were unlikely to use the tunnel cited claustrophobia as a factor influencing their decision
- 31 per cent said they would prefer to use the tunnel if taking a car abroad, citing speed and convenience of travel as influential factors (the tunnel is expected to take 35 minutes to cross compared with 75 minutes by ferry).

These findings are significant within a marketing context for Eurotunnel as they imply that the company is not communicating effectively with potential tourists who may choose to travel via the tunnel. This is contributing to the tunnel's weakness as a new entrant to the cross-Channel market, while the ferry operators have responded to the immediate threat of the tunnel by enhancing

Case study 3 (*continued*)

their marketing activities and public image to raise awareness of their service.

One initial strategy pursued by P & O European Ferries (hereafter P & O) and Stena Sealink was to consider the feasibility of developing a joint shuttle service with common price structures

Table 2.4 An analysis of strengths, weaknesses, opportunities and threats for cross-Channel ferries

Strengths	Weaknesses	Opportunities	Threats
Choice of routes	Frequency of services	The cross-Channel market is growing	Poor surface links to some ports
Opportunity for on-board leisure	Cannot offer city centre to city centre services	Ferry companies are upgrading their product	Immigration will not be juxtaposed as for tunnel
Opportunities for scheduled breaks for drivers	Poor baggage handling for foot passengers	Improved port handling facilities	Potential loss of duty-free sales (subject to a future decision by the EC)
Access to scenery and fresh air	Perceived problem of adverse weather conditions	Easier booking facilities	High-quality and continental tourist attractions
Advance booking and strong links with travel agents	Longer crossing time	Improved reservation system and common ticketing	Widespread publicity about the tunnel
On-board business centres	Lack of co-ordination between ferry and rail services		Novelty appeal of the tunnel
Sea crossing is often one of Britain's attractions for continental leisure visitors			
Can carry cars/coaches/commercial vehicles			

Source: British Tourist Authority (1991) *1993 Cross-Channel Marketing Strategy.*
Copyright: British Tourist Authority.

Case study 3 (*continued*)

Table 2.5 An analysis of strengths, weaknesses, opportunities and threats for Eurotunnel's proposed shuttle service

Strengths	Weaknesses	Opportunities	Threats
Frequency of services	Limited on-board leisure experience	Novelty appeal of tunnel travel	High-quality mainland European tourist attractions
Shorter Channel crossing time	No experience of ticket sales and dealing with the travel trade	Widespread publicity	Fear of travelling in a tunnel beneath the Channel
Unaffected by adverse weather conditions	No access to scenery or fresh air	The cross-Channel market is growing	Inadequate road links, causing congestion problems
Can carry cars/ coaches/ commercial vehicles	No choice for cross-Channel route	Many mainland Europeans perceive the Channel as a barrier to spontaneous travel which the tunnel will overcome	Fear of terrorist attacks
Perceived as an extension to mainland European motorways		Attracting holiday, business and VFR travellers	No duty-free sales
Juxtaposed immigration procedures			

Source: British Tourist Authority (1991) *1993 Cross-Channel Marketing Strategy.*
Copyright: British Tourist Authority.

between Dover and Calais for car ferries. In 1989 the Monopolies and Mergers Commission's (MMC) report 'Cross-Channel Car Ferries' (Cmd. 584, HMSO) considered that their proposal was against the public interest. This reaffirmed the Monopolies Commission decision in 1974 which prevented a revenue-pooling cartel for cross-Channel ferries. However, one note of optimism

Case study 3 (*continued*)

was that the MMC report in 1989 did not preclude a further application to operate joint services near the tunnel's opening date, although this was rejected again in 1992. However, recent transport analysts have cast doubt on the viability of such a proposal, since P & O and Sealink are not compatible partners, the latter requiring significant restructuring to reach the level of efficiency in ferry operations achieved by P & O since 1988.

Whilst the discussions of joint services continued, individual ferry companies operating services on the short-sea sector have also pursued major capital investment programmes in larger vessels to achieve economies of scale and to improve the quality of service in the later 1980s and 1990s. For example, new on-board services and facilities, such as Club Class for business travellers on P & O, the provision of motorist lounges, restaurants, eating facilities, entertainment centres and opportunities for tax- and duty-free shopping have significantly improved the sea-borne experience for tourist travel. There has also been a greater degree of segmentation to develop niche markets (e.g. short-break motoring holidays and Eurodisney packages). As a result, the threat of the Channel Tunnel has led to major improvements for cross-Channel tourist travel with increased choice, greater competition and improved quality of service. Marketing has played a major part by communicating these changes to the tourist to develop customer loyalty, increased levels of satisfaction from the travel experience and to ensure future patronage. The tunnel has meant that the combination of strategic planning and marketing research has been harnessed by ferry operators to develop a concerted response in the competitive business environment of the 1990s.

Marketing research

This process is one which is often seen as synonymous with market research but as the following definition by Seibert (1973) implies, in reality it is a much broader concept as 'marketing research is an organised process associated with the gathering, processing, analysis, storage and dissemination of information to facilitate and improve decision-making'.

It incorporates various forms of research undertaken by organisations to understand their customers, markets and business efficiency. The actual research methods used to investigate different aspects of a company's business ultimately determine the type of research undertaken. The main types of research can be summarised into six categories (see Table 2.6). A number of good introductions to marketing research are available and more recent books on tourism research are recommended as preliminary reading on this topic (e.g. Witt and Moutinho 1989; Veal 1992). Marketing research allows the company to keep in touch with its customers to monitor needs and tastes which are constantly changing in time and space. However, the actual implementation of marketing for tourist transport ultimately depends on the 'marketing mix'.

Table 2.6 Categories of marketing research

Research category	Used in	Typical marketing use
1. Marketing analysis and forecasting	Marketing planning	Measurement and projections of market volumes, shares and revenue by relevant categories of market segments and product types
2. Consumer research	Segmentation and positioning	(a) Quantitative measurement of consumer profiles, awareness attitudes and purchasing behaviour including consumer audits (b) Qualitative assessments of consumer needs, perceptions and aspirations
3. Products and price studies	Product formulation, presentation and pricing	Measurement and consumer testing of amended and new product formulations, and price-sensitivity studies
4. Promotions and sales research	Efficiency of communications	Measurement of consumer reaction to alternative concepts and media usage; response to various forms of sales promotion, and sales force effectiveness
5. Distribution research	Efficiency of distribution network	Distributor awareness of products, stocking and display of brochures, and effectiveness of merchandising, including retail audits and occupancy studies
6. Evaluation and performance-monitoring studies	Overall control of marketing results	Measurement of customer satisfaction overall, and by product elements, including measurement through marketing tests and experiments

Source: Middleton (1988: 109).

The marketing mix

The marketing mix is 'the mixture of controllable marketing variables that the firm [or company] uses to pursue the sought level of sales in the target market' (Kotler cited in Holloway and Plant 1988: 48). This means that for a given tourist transport organisation such as an airline, there are four main marketing variables which it needs to harness to achieve the goals identified in the marketing strategy formulated through the strategic planning process. These variables are:

- *Product formulation* – which is the ability of a company to adapt to the needs of its customers in terms of the services it provides. These are constantly being adapted to changes in consumer markets.
- *Price* – is the economic concept used to adjust the supply of a service to meet the demand, taking account of sales targets and turnover.
- *Promotion* – is the manner in which a company seeks to improve customers' knowledge of the services it sells so that those people who are made aware may be turned into actual purchasers. To achieve promotional aims, advertising, public relations, sales and brochure production functions are undertaken within this remit as promotion. Not surprisingly promotion often consumes the largest proportion of marketing budgets.
- *Place* – this refers to the location at which prospective customers may be induced to purchase a service – the point of sale (e.g. a travel agent).

As marketing variables, production, price, promotion and place are normally called the four 'Ps'. These are incorporated into the marketing process in relation to the known competition and the impact of market conditions. Thus, the marketing process involves the continuous evaluation of how a business operates internally and externally and it can be summarised as 'the management process which identifies, anticipates and supplies customers' requirements efficiently and profitably' (UK Institute of Marketing, cited in Cannon 1989).

Within the context of tourist transport, marketing has a certain degree of synergy with economics as an understanding of economic concepts and the way in which the marketplace works is fundamental to marketing. But the application of marketing principles to the tourist transport system requires one to recognise that we are dealing with a service (see Kotler and Armstrong 1991) and the tourist experience which is embodied in the concept of the service encounter.

For this reason, attention now turns to marketing tourist transport as a service.

Tourist transport as a service

Gilbert (1989) notes the growing importance of service quality and consumer satisfaction in tourism in the late 1980s. In the context of tourist transport, what is meant by a service? Defining the term 'service' is difficult owing to the intangibility, perishability and inseparability of services. Kotler and Armstrong (1991: 620) define the three terms as follows:

- Service intangibility – a service is something which cannot be seen, tasted, felt, heard or smelt before it is purchased.
- Service perishability – a service cannot be stored for sale or used at a later date.
- Service inseparability – a service is usually produced and consumed at the same time and cannot be separated from providers.

Van Dierdonck (1992) argues that the intangible nature of a service is determined by the fact that unlike manufactured goods, a service is provided and consumed at the same time and same place, making it difficult to define and communicate its form to customers. Even so, it is possible to identify six core elements in a service if it is defined as a product, where each element affects customer perception of the service:

- the image of the service
- the image of personnel with whom customers interact
- image differences within the same sectors of the service provider (e.g. how does a service compare with that offered by competitors?)
- the customer group targeted
- the influence of the physical environment in which the service is delivered (e.g. the building)
- the working atmosphere in which the service is formulated, designed and delivered.
  (Modified from Flipo, cited in Van Dierdonck 1992.)

An alternative view of a service is that it constitutes a process rather than an end product, which actually disappears once it has been made. In this respect, a service can be conceptualised as a process which responds to the diverse needs of consumers. Since consumers are not homogeneous it is difficult to standardise a product to meet every need.

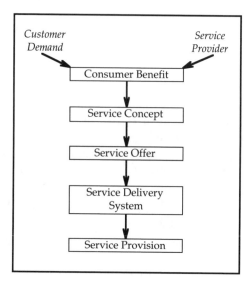

Figure 2.6 The service process
Source: After Cowell (1986).

The process of providing a service which tailors something to meet precise and varied needs is integral to the concept of responsive service provision.

Researchers such as Poon (1989) have argued that the challenge for tourism-related enterprises, such as transport providers, is to respond to the growing sophistication of tourists so that the entire tourism experience meets the expectations of the consumer. In this context, three key issues which emerge are service quality, customer care and the service encounter (Gilbert 1989). From the consumer's perspective, the use of critical incidents (Bitner *et al.* 1990) in the service process (e.g. where the service delivery breaks down) has been used to analyse the consumer's service encounter and how they view it under adverse conditions.

If we accept that there is a consensus among marketing researchers that service provision needs to be seen as an ongoing process, how does this process operate? Cowell (1986) examined this process as a four-stage system (see Figure 2.6) with the provider trying to offer a service in response to actual or perceived customer demand. The process is based on the following concepts:

The consumer benefit   At the outset, the supplier of a service tries to understand what the consumer wants and how they may benefit from the service. At this stage, a detailed understanding of consumer behaviour is required which recognises the relative importance of those factors influencing the purchase decision (Qaiters and Bergiel 1989). These include social, economic, cultural, business and family influences and how these condition and affect attitudes, motives, needs and perception of consumers. In the case of tourist transport services, a significant amount of research on the social psychology of tourists has examined what holidays tourists choose, the mode of transport selected and the factors affecting their decision-making as consumers (Javalgi *et al*. 1992; Mansfeld 1992). Following the consumer benefit stage, the service provider translates the assessment of consumer demands into a *service concept*.

The service concept   At this point, the supplier examines the means of producing a service and how it will be distributed to consumers. Marketing research at both the *consumer benefit* and *service concept* stage is essential to assist in identifying the specific market segment to target and the nature of the consumer/producer relationship (e.g. is the service to be sold direct to the public or via a different distribution channel such as a travel agent?). Lastly, the producer identifies and develops the image which is to be associated with the service. Having established what the service will comprise in concept form, it is developed further into the *service offer*.

The service offer   At this point, the service concept is given more shape and developed within precise terms set by managerial decisions which specify:

- the elements – the ingredients
- the form – how it will be offered to consumers
- the levels of service – what the consumer will expect to receive in terms of the quality and quantity of the service.

The composition of the service elements is discussed in detail by Gronroos (1980). The form of the service concept also needs to be considered in terms of how the corporate image will be communicated to the public. Furthermore the service levels, the technical aspects of service quality and how it is rendered also need to be assessed as part of the *service offer*.

Despite the significance of the *service offer* there is little evidence available to suggest that consumers judge service quality in a definitive way. For example, Lovelock (1992a, b) acknowledges that services such as tourist transport, which have a high degree of customer contact, need to be recognised when entering the last stage – *service delivery*.

The service delivery system   This is the system which is developed to deliver the service to the customer and will comprise both the people responsible for different aspects of the service experience and the physical evidence such as the transport and environment in which it is delivered (Bitner 1992). The tourist's experience of these components is embodied in the *service encounter* (Laws 1991). It is the service delivery system where barriers may occur in the provision of a satisfactory encounter (see Thornberry and Hennessey 1992) and one to which a great deal of marketing research has been directed to identify deficiencies, critical incidents and ways of overcoming dissatisfaction (Bitner *et al.* 1990). The pursuit of excellence in service delivery (Peters and Waterman 1982; Berry and Parasuraman 1991) has meant companies monitoring what the consumer wants and then providing it. In this context marketing assumes a critical role both in terms of research and communication with customers. By providing quality in service provision, it may help to develop customer loyalty in the patronage of tourist transport. As the competitive market for tourist transport intensifies, the demand for service delivery systems which are customer centred are likely to be important factors in affecting tourist use of transport services. The consumer is a key player in the service process, being an active participant and important judge of quality (Zeithmal and Berry 1985).

Summary

This chapter has shown that three social science subjects (economics, geography and marketing) have developed a range of concepts and distinctive approaches to the analysis of different aspects of the tourist transport system. The case studies of New Zealand, Ireland and cross-Channel travel have highlighted how these concepts can help us to understand different features of the tourist travel experience and the interaction of the consumer and producer in tourist transport systems. The economists' analysis of tourist transport systems is based on the demand and supply issues associated with the use and provision of different modes of transport and the implications for the future (i.e. forecasting, which is dealt with in Chapter 4). In contrast, the geographer has largely focused on the spatial analysis, organisation and distribution of tourist patterns of travel while the transport geographer has considered the policy, management and planning issues associated with the provision of transport, sometimes in combination with economists (see the contributions in Banister and Button 1992). In marketing, the interest in tourist transport is poorly developed within the existing literature, although the contribution should not be understated because marketers have identified the importance of a more consumer-oriented focus for tourist transport provision. The concern for service quality which has emerged in the marketing literature has started to permeate tourist transport provision, particularly in the airline sector (see Laws 1991 for a fuller discussion) which is explored further in Chapter 3.

It is clear from the discussion of the contribution made by economists, geographers and marketers in the analysis of tourist transport systems that these need to be integrated into a more coherent framework which is possible by adopting a systems approach. In reality, the decision-making functions undertaken by transport operators and public sector organisations associated with tourism and transport invariably use a variety of economic, geographical and marketing principles in their everyday work to plan and develop tourist transport services. The concern with enhancing the tourists' travel experience, so that it meets with the preconceived notion of service quality and provision, has become a concern not only for operators but also for government policy-making. It is the issue of government policy-making and its effect on tourist transport systems which is the focus of the next chapter.

Questions

1 What concepts characterise the economists', geographers' and marketers' analysis of tourist transport?
2 Prepare a SWOT analysis for a tourist transport service you are familiar with.
3 What type of market research would you undertake to assess why tourists choose to travel on specific forms of transport?
4 Evaluate the quality of provision for a tourist transport system you have used.

Further reading

Boniface, C. and Cooper, C. (1987) *The Geography of Travel and Tourism*, London: Heinemann.

Churchill, G.A. (1992) *Basic Marketing Research*, Fort Worth: Dryden Press.

Gray, H.P. (1982) 'The contribution of economics to tourism', *Annals of Tourism Research* 9: 105–25.

Holloway, J.C. and Plant, R.V. (1988) *Marketing for Tourism*, London: Pitman.

Mansfeld, Y. (1990) 'Spatial patterns of international tourist flows: towards a theoretical approach', *Progress in Human Geography* 14, 3: 372–90.

Page, S. (1994) 'The European coach travel market', *Travel and Tourism Analyst* 1: 19–39.

Peel, M. (1988) *Customer Service: How to Achieve Total Customer Satisfaction*, London: Kogan Page.

3
Tourist transport and government policy

Introduction

Transport results from a desire for mobility and travel, and the provision of different modes of transport aims to facilitate the efficient movement of goods and people. To provide a framework in which these objectives can be achieved, national governments formulate policies to guide the organisation, management and development of tourist and non-tourist transportation (Starkie 1976; Knowles 1989). The transport policies developed by national governments are influenced by their changing attitudes, outlook and political ideology which directly affect tourist travel in terms of capital investment, infrastructure provision and policies to *facilitate* (Department of Employment/English Tourist Board 1991) or *constrain* tourist travel (see Griffith's 1989 discussion of international airways sanctions against South Africa). Transport policy has a direct bearing on the development and promotion of tourism, and as the UK's Department of Transport recognised,

> tourism and leisure depend heavily on travel and transport. In Britain, travelling by road represents the dominant mode for visitors to get to and from their final destinations or to see places of interest . . . [and] . . . the tourism industry, in common with many other industries, also depends heavily on roads for the transport of the goods and services people need.
>
> (Department of Transport 1987: 1)

while the Republic of Ireland's Department of Transport and Tourism acknowledges that:

> the development of an enhanced internal transport network fully integrated with appropriate access infrastructure and services is a fundamental requirement for the future development of the tourism industry. This requires the provision of good quality access transport services and facilities together with a satisfactory internal transport infrastructure and services.
>
> (Government of Ireland 1990: 24)

Although these statements highlight the inter-related nature of transport and tourism, in practice the responsibility for transport and tourism is often in different government departments, and where little inter-department liaison occurs, there is poor co-ordination of policies affecting tourist transport (see Banister and Hall 1981 for a public policy perspective).

Public sector involvement in the tourist transport system at national government level is designed to facilitate, control and in some cases regulate or deregulate the activities of private sector transport operators with a view to 'looking after the public's interests and providing goods whose costs cannot readily be attributed to groups or individuals' (Pearce 1990: 32; see also Chapter 5 on airline deregulation). Since the private sector's primary role is revenue generation and profit maximisation from the tourist transport system, the government's role is to promote and protect the interest of the consumer against unfair business practices, and to ensure safety standards are maintained to protect the interests of employees in large- and small-scale transport operations.

In this chapter, the role of government policy in regulating tourist transport provision and the effect upon different modes of tourist transport is examined. The chapter discusses the concept of transport policy, its meaning and the political variants of transport policy in a free market economy. The significance of transnational organisations such as the EC and their progress towards a Common Transport Policy for rail travel is examined given the expected renaissance in tourist rail travel in the 1990s. This is followed by a discussion of government policy towards tourist and non-tourist rail travel in the UK. What is meant by transport policy?

The role of government and tourist transport policy

The term 'policy' is frequently used to denote the direction and objectives an organisation wishes to pursue over a set period of time. In the case of transport, national policy is normally formulated by government organisations with economic and social factors in mind, without an explicit concern for tourism even though transport networks are used for tourist and non-tourist travel. The development and shape of transport policy is partly affected by the existing infrastructure which has resulted from major public and private sector investment to achieve general and specific transport objectives. Transport policy may also be influenced by other government policies such as defence, and in some cases former defence infrastructure has been given over to civilian uses. Changes to the underlying infrastructure cannot be exacted quickly owing to the major capital costs, planning procedures and the time delay in responding to the demand for new infrastructure. For example, the expansion of an airport to accommodate a forecast growth in tourist arrivals may take between 5 and 10 years from its inception to the completion stage. Significant changes can occur quickly in relation to the licensing of tourist transport to increase capacity as illustrated in Chapter 2 with the case study of New Zealand, where an increase in the supply of international flights facilitated an expansion in the latent demand for tourist travel. Even so, these changes have to be set against the increased environmental impact (e.g. noise, pollution, waste and greater numbers of tourists – see Chapter 6) resulting from additional flights (see Somerville 1992). Transport policy is not always a passive or reactive element of government activity as changes in society and the demand for tourist and non-tourist travel require a certain degree of continuity and change in policy to meet new trends and activity patterns among the population. What political and ideological principles affect transport policy?

National transport policies have been characterised by a range of approaches which span a spectrum from a free market orientation to those based on planned resource allocation (Farrington 1985). The market-oriented view has been pursued on the premise that centralised state control of transportation produces an unwieldy and often unresponsive service requiring unnecessarily high subsidies from state taxation. By introducing a greater degree of private sector involvement and competition, it is argued that improved services should result and the need for public subsidies should diminish. In contrast, supporters of the regulated planned response towards state involvement in transportation have pointed to classical economic theory which recognises that in a free market economy, supply imperfections result. State intervention in the market economy is justified to rectify supply imperfections on social efficiency and environmental grounds to avoid inequalities in accessibility. In situations where inadequate levels of demand exist to support a viable service, state subsidies may be required to provide access for communities on social grounds (Whitelegg 1987). Thus government intervention in transport activities, either directly or through other agencies to co-ordinate different parts of the transport system, is essential to bring order to the different components of the system so that they operate in harmony. The level of intervention needed to achieve this co-ordinating function depends on the political views of the government and its policy objectives, which are subject to the changing attitudes and external influences upon policy formulation. Therefore, how have these principles been applied to transport policy in the past and what effect have they had on the tourist transport system?

Historical interpretations of transport policy: implications for tourist travel

According to Button and Gillingwater (1983), in Europe and North America transport policy has affected the tourist transport system in a number of ways although it is based on two underlying economic principles:

- allocative efficiency (the use of resources and the price mechanism to achieve the efficient access to transport and travel)
- political obligations (the need for the state to protect the public interest in transport provision).

These principles have had an important effect on the provision of transport for tourist travel in terms of the development, expansion and regulation of different modes of transport to facilitate access to tourism resources. Modes of transport which enable mass travel developed at different times in Europe and North America but the effects were similar in terms of making tourist travel more available. Technological innovations and their commercial exploitation (e.g. the motor car), and their diffusion to different social groups during the late nineteenth and twentieth centuries, have been shaped by transport policy to achieve the twin goals of allocative efficiency and political obligations.

In historical terms, the principles of allocative efficiency and political obligations have been interpreted in different ways by governments and Button and Gillingwater (1983) identify four distinct phases in transport policy:

- *The Railway Age* which, in the UK, led to heavy investment in the provision of infrastructure that made seaside resorts accessible to the working classes after the 1870s. Government promotion of railways in the private sector dominated the period, except during the wartime period (1914–18) when state control emerged to co-ordinate and manage the railways in the 'national interest' of efficiency.
- *The Age of Protection*, which characterised the 1920s and 1930s, saw the emergence of road transport, particularly the rise of the private car and coach travel in an unplanned manner. This led governments to intervene in the marketplace to avoid massive cost cutting among private operators as competition intensified due to the growing number of small transport operators. Such intervention was justified on the basis that the effects of major competition may have led to a reduction in the number of operators, following a price war to secure passengers and market share. It was expected that this would be followed by a much reduced route network and poorer level of service. In the USA, this was characterised by the 1935 Motor Carriage Act which protected the Greyhound Bus Operations, providing one major operator with a virtual monopoly on inter-urban bus travel.
- *The Age of Administrative Planning*, which emerged in the post-war period (i.e. after 1945) and superseded the Age of Protection, saw the private car emerge as a portent force for tourist and recreational travel. One consequence was the growing financial weakness of railways, although urban growth continued to dictate the need for large, efficient, urban passenger transport systems. The nationalisation of railway networks and other forms of public transport epitomise this era in transport policy. The 1960s saw a growing burden of state subsidies to support public transport and some attempts to restructure the transport network radically (e.g. the Beeching Report in the UK and subsequent rationalisation of the rail network). In the UK, the 1968 Transport Act sought to reorganise public transport and one consequence for tourist travel was the establishment of the National Bus Company, with the responsibility for express coach travel. In the USA, the 1962 Urban Mass Transportation Act pro-

vided Federal Grants for two-thirds of public transport projects. Efficiency in provision was interpreted by government policy in terms of integration and co-ordination of transport planning which reduced wasteful competition (Button and Gillingwater 1983).

- *The Age of Contestability* has characterised the period since the early 1970s in the USA (and the 1980s in the UK), based on the pursuit of the principle of deregulation to achieve 'allocative efficiency in transport policy' (Farrington 1985). By creating efficient transport operations and reducing public subsidies, the private sector is seen as the main panacea for efficient transport operations (Knowles and Hall 1992). In the UK the sale of the state-owned airline – British Airways – and its emergence as a profitable private sector company is cited as one of the main successes of privatisation and deregulation by supporters of this political philosophy. It is interesting to note that the UK/North American experience in transport policy in the 1970s and 1980s has not been adopted and endorsed in many other European countries where the state remains committed to investment in tourist transport systems. However, the Age of Contestability may have some significance for transnational organisations, such as the EC, where the Single European Act has sought to introduce greater competition and a reduction in state subsidies to achieve greater efficiency in transport provision. Even this is not without problems as the example of the Common Transport Policy for rail travel indicates.

A Common Transport Policy for rail travel in the EC

Rail transport and rail networks are state owned in all member states of the EC, and they receive subsidies to assist with the operation of uneconomic services. Yet there are certain European governments (e.g. the UK and Sweden) which have sought to introduce greater competition, aspects of privatisation and a more explicit market orientation for rail passenger transport after many years of state control. As Page (1993d) notes, state ownership of rail transport has produced organisations managing national railway networks which are characterised by:

- a close relationship with central government due to state ownership and the provision of operating subsidies
- periodic changes in the political will of national governments to subsidise rail

- constraints on investment planning and a forward-looking approach to development
- a lack of management freedom prior to the 1980s
- an inability to prevent loss of market share in rail travel in the 1970s and early 1980s.

The close relationship between the management of railways and the interests of national governments has meant that policy-making has been largely inward looking and focused on national rather than EC-wide concerns. Gibb and Charlton (1992) have confirmed this view in their analysis of the EC's role as an organisation intended to foster co-operation in transport policy among the member states of the Community. They found that in the case of rail travel, the wider considerations of the EC have been undermined by the vested interests of national governments in their own rail networks. As a result, the EC has made little progress towards developing a common rail policy owing to two principal objectives of EC transport policy which consistently cause conflict:

- the desire to liberalise rail transport to achieve free trade policies in the move towards the Single European Market,[1] and
- the need to harmonise the conditions of competition in rail services in pursuit of social intervention policies.

The EC 'Proposal for a Council Directive on the Development of Community Railways' (COM (89) 564 final), which was finalised in July 1991, embodied these principles. It proposed that railway operations and infrastructure should be the responsibility of two separate organisations, so that railway companies can make commercial decisions about long-distance passenger services. This is designed to facilitate an expansion in international rail passenger services where the user entering a national network pays a user-fee, thereby reducing the possibility of cross-subsidisation of railway networks by national governments. While the EC aimed to introduce freedom of access to national railway networks across the Community, the changes required by national governments to achieve these objectives imply an end to the highly regulated environment in which state-managed railway enterprises operate. To date, there has been a failure to agree the principles necessary to develop a Common Transport Policy, and rail transport is no exception to this. The prospects for providing access to national railway networks and the introduction of competitive operations is highly speculative owing to the challenge to existing national markets and services. In the absence of an EC Common Transport Policy what should be the main components of an effective state policy for tourist transport?

The Organisation for Economic Development and Cooperation (OECD) has argued that effective state policies for tourist transport should be integrated so that both tourism and transport concerns work in harmony rather than in isolation. Transport policy needs to consider tourism as a related activity which is directly influenced by the objectives pursued in national and regional transport policy. In fact Sinclair and Page (1993) examine the role of policy formulation in a transfrontier region (the Euroregion – in north east France and south east England) in relation to transport, tourism and regional development. This is an interesting example where cross-border co-operation and planning for transport may assist in co-ordinating the variety of bodies involved in implementing tourism and transport planning in two different countries. It also illustrates how a wider policy-making framework can assist in the recognition of the vital link between transport planning and tourism to promote economic development in local areas.

Yet translating policy objectives into a planning framework may pose particular problems for tourist transport systems since the political philosophy of national governments can lead to different approaches as to who funds and develops transport infrastructure projects. For example, many airports are now commercially operated enterprises, a principle established in the UK government's White Paper *Airports Policy* (HMSO 1978) which was mirrored in many other European countries (see Doganis 1992). In this respect, infrastructure provision is now based in the private sector with the UK government's market-led philosophy also applying to complementary infrastructure provision. For example, this is demonstrated by the planned public:private sector partnership between BR and the British Airports Authority's £300 million Heathrow Express rail-link project to connect Heathrow and Paddington in London.

Where countries do formulate a tourist transport policy, its implementation through planning measures needs to consider the following issues:

- the management of tourist traffic in large urban areas (see the London Tourist Board 1990: 61–3, on managing transport used by visitors, particularly the problem of coach parking which is also discussed by the Bus and Coach Council 1991) and small historic cities (see Page 1992b for a case study of Canterbury)

- the management of tourist and recreational traffic in rural areas (see Sharpley 1993 for an up to date assessment)
- the promotion of off-peak travel by tourists to spread the seasonal and geographical distribution of tourist travel and the resulting economic, social and cultural impacts of tourism
- maximising the use of existing transport infrastructure and the use of more novel forms of tourist transport and the provision of new infrastructure on the basis of long-term traffic forecasts.

With these issues in mind, attention now turns to a case study of the state's role in tourist transport to assess which objectives are being pursued towards tourist rail travel in the UK.

Case study 4: The organisation and management of a tourist transport system: tourist rail travel in the United Kingdom

In this case study, the organisation and management of a tourist transport service – rail travel – is examined to illustrate how government transport policy has a direct and indirect impact on a tourist transport system. The case study develops the idea of a system introduced in Chapter 1, to show how government policy and regulation affects the provision and consumption of a service for tourists which operates as an integrated system. In this system, the main input comprises the supply of a service by BR and the demand for tourist travel while the principal output comprises the tourist travel experience as a service encounter (see Figure 3.1), thereby introducing some of the ideas and concepts developed in Chapter 2. The nature and organisation of this system of tourist travel is indicated in Figure 3.1 which identifies the inter-relationships between the provider of the service and the purchaser (i.e. the tourist). As Figure 3.1 shows, a complex set of relationships affects the supply and demand for tourist travel by rail, with a variety of organisations directly affecting the supply via regulatory and financial controls (e.g. Department of Transport and the Treasury). However, prior to discussing the role of the state in policy formation and its implementation, it is useful to

Case study 4 (*continued*)

---

establish the dimensions of the supply and demand for tourist rail travel in the UK.

Tourist travel by rail in the UK

Turton (1992a) examines the role of rail passenger transport in the UK, providing a broad overview of the various factors which affect the organisation and management of passenger services, the impact of government policy and the relative importance of rail versus other modes of transport. The UK rail network comprises 16,585 route kilometres and some 740 million passenger journeys were undertaken in 1991/2. Potter (1987) argues that the main determinants of the demand for rail travel are:

- speed
- cost
- comfort
- convenience
- access to stations
- the image of the service

These affect the perceived quality of the service and are often judged in relation to competing modes of transport.

In terms of tourist demand, Turton (1991) reports that the Long Distance Travel Survey (1979–80) found that rail had a 20 per cent share of all long-distance trips (those over 40 km). According to Jefferson and Lickorish (1991), the number of domestic tourists using rail to reach their holiday destination in Great Britain has dropped from 13 per cent in 1971 to 10 per cent in 1985 and 8 per cent in 1989. For journeys to the European mainland which included a sea crossing, 8 per cent of British tourists travelled by BR in 1986. In 1991/2, the business traveller using InterCity comprised:

- 23 per cent of InterCity passenger volumes
- 35 per cent of receipts and
- approximately 8 per cent of the UK long-distance travel market.

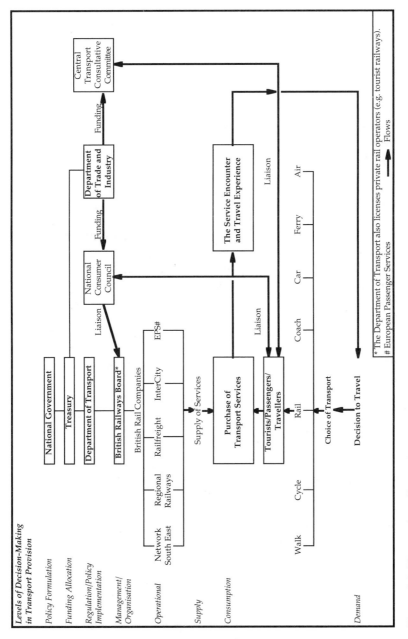

Figure 3.1 The tourist rail travel system in the UK

Case study 4 (*continued*)

Rail travel in the UK has seen a significant drop in public support
and patronage since the 1970s as competition with other modes of
transport (e.g. air, car and coach travel) have eroded rail's market
share. How far is this a result of government policy as opposed to
changing attitudes and preferences among travellers, and to what
extent is the decline in the use of rail for tourist trips a unique
feature in the UK? (See Page 1993d for a discussion of the
situation in other European countries.) For example, in the 1970s
and early 1980s, BR penetrated the domestic long-distance holiday
market, selling over 170,000 'Golden Rail Holidays' per annum in
the late 1980s (Lavery 1989) but its share of the long-distance
travel market continued to decline, despite attempts to diversify its
product base. A significant proportion of tourists in the UK use
trunk rail routes (Figure 3.2) and inter-urban travel dominate the
traffic flows (Turton 1992b) since much of the demand emanated
from the main towns and cities, which also contain many of the
UK's main tourist gateways. Those rail routes which experienced
the greatest volume of traffic were the electrified east and west
coast main lines, linking London and Scotland with many of the
UK's major towns and cities. Feeder services from rural areas to
the main trunk routes and cross-country express services during
periods of peak demand (e.g. summer services from inland towns
and cities to coastal resorts) provide additional services connecting
most destinations to the rail network.[2] Prideaux (1990) notes that
the demand for InterCity rail travel in 1989 was 8.5 million passengers who travelled 77 million journeys. Within the overall demand,
different segments are discernible (e.g. youth travel, business
travellers, the elderly and disabled), each of which generates its
own patterns of demand. The provision of such rail services is
subject to the prevailing policy objectives of the national government, with the Department of Transport responsible for the implementation of the policy.

Case study 4 (*continued*)

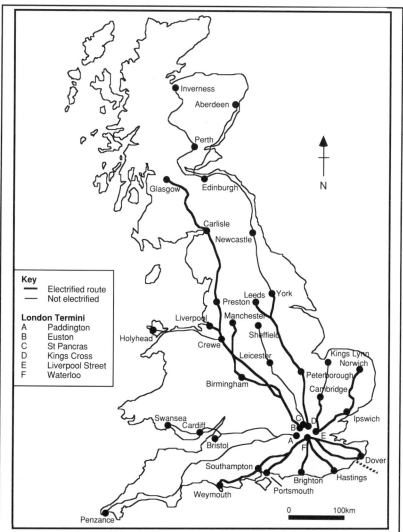

Figure 3.2 UK trunk rail routes

Note: This simplified map of principal trunk lines does not include cross-country services operated by regional railways, cross-country Intercity holidaymaker services, cross-London Thameslink services or the London Underground Ltd network serving London.

Case study 4 (*continued*)

Government regulation of rail services in the UK: the Department of Transport

The Department of Transport is the government department responsible for regulating rail travel and it licenses a number of tourist railways, many of which are operated on a seasonal basis to meet the demand for scenic and nostalgic journeys (Holloway 1989). Since 1981, government policy in the UK has rolled back the role of the state in the regulation of public transport through selective measures of privatisation (e.g. the 1985 Transport Act – Knowles 1985, 1989) in an attempt to develop a greater degree of commercialism in service provision (e.g. the sale of BR's ferry operations – Sealink – to the private sector in 1984), while BR's government subsidy was cut by 60 per cent between 1983 and 1989. For BR, this has meant that it has had to adopt a greater degree of market-led planning towards rail services.

Rail privatisation in the UK

The Department of Transport has announced its plans to implement government policy objectives – to introduce further measures to privatise the railway system (Department of Transport 1992a, 1992b, 1993). These plans embody the ideological stance of the government towards the level of state intervention necessary in the transport system. The government's intention is to pursue the objective of minimum public subsidy for rail travel with a view to proceeding with measures which would have private rail services operational by 1994, using a hybrid solution which introduces private sector investment and expertise into railway businesses and leads to a radical overhaul of its management and organisation. It has resulted in the establishment of 'Railtrack', a company responsible for operating infrastructure, and another company responsible for overseeing passenger services until they are franchised out. This may end BR's 44 year role as the main provider of rail services, in an attempt to improve efficiency and introduce competition

Case study 4 (*continued*)

(European Conference of Ministers of Transport 1992). Recent studies have examined the utility of such an approach (e.g. Adamson *et al*.1991) and critics of privatisation have argued that lack of government investment is responsible for the poor performance of the nationalised railway company. Yet within the European railway industry, it is widely acknowledged that BR operates one of the most efficient railway networks in Europe, in view of the level of staffing and government subsidy provided per passenger kilometres travelled. Even so, the government has also encouraged public service providers such as BR to improve service quality and to establish a Passenger's Charter following the launch of the Citizen's Charter initiative in 1991 (National Consumer Council 1991). Two other statutory organisations also influence the provision of rail services – the Central Transport Consultative Committee (CTCC) and the National Consumer Council (NCC) (see Figure 3.1) – while other pressure groups and organisations lobby for improvements to rail services for tourists.

British Railways and rail service provision

The majority of long-distance tourist trips by rail in the UK are undertaken on InterCity and to a lesser extent on regional railways, which compete with the express coach business and domestic airlines for business and leisure travel. In a climate of reducing government subsidy for rail travel, BR did achieve a complete reversal in InterCity's financial performance from a £157 million loss on £623 million passenger revenue in 1987/8 to a £324 million profit on passenger revenue of £725 million in 1988/9. In 1991/2, InterCity's income was £896.7 million, with £829.7 million from passenger fares, £45.3 million from non-fare income (e.g. catering) and £21.7 million from ancillary services. In the medium to long term, however, the real potential for BR to expand its market share of long-distance tourist travel lies in the European passenger services running from London to mainland Europe through the Channel Tunnel (Page and Sinclair 1992a, b).

Case study 4 (*continued*)

British Rail and the customer: the tourist travel experience and service encounter

For the tourist, the journey on a train represents the consumption of a travel service. From a tourism perspective, this is the culmination of the desire to travel and the selection of a mode of transport to fulfil that need (Figure 3.1). Recent researchers such as Poon (1989) acknowledge the growing sophistication of tourists and their higher expectations from travel and tourism services. For the supplier, it has led to a much greater focus on service quality. Within BR, those sectors which deal with leisure and business travellers on a regular basis (e.g. InterCity) have recognised the need to provide a consistent level of service which meets the expectations of customers. This service encounter begins at the point when the ticket is purchased and includes the time spent waiting at the station through to the completion of the journey. The experience on-board the train is also deemed to be one of the most memorable aspects of the journey and an integral part of the service encounter. Shilton (1982) suggests that while it is difficult to quantify the quality aspects of InterCity services, factors such as the condition of the rolling stock, the image of the high-speed trains and additional advertising accounted for half of the increased patronage of the long-distance travel market in the early 1980s. InterCity has also been conscious of the need to expand its share of tourist and non-tourist high-speed rail travel in the long-distance travel market by introducing new products (e.g. Family Railcards), cultivating niche markets such as off-peak premium travel (e.g. 'Weekend First' – discounted first-class travel) as well as budget advance purchase (Apex) tickets. As two-thirds of InterCity's business travellers chose second-class (standard) accommodation (Prideaux 1990), InterCity introduced the 'Silver Standard' service for full-fare standard-class passengers. This includes free seat reservations, complimentary airline-style meals and steward service and is a deliberate attempt to offer a competitive service equivalent to that currently provided by domestic airlines.

Case study 4 (*continued*)

The demand for enhanced service quality on InterCity services among more discerning travellers has meant that new services have been provided for different market segments. In addition, the quality and ease of interchange facilities at major rail termini in the UK (e.g. at the ports, airports and in major cities) are important factors affecting the tourist's travel experience and may influence the decision to travel by train.

Interchanges need to be integrated with easy access to other modes of transport for onward travel so that the commencement and completion of the journey are not marred by difficulties in making connections. One further development which has a wide-ranging impact on the service quality of tourist use of rail is the introduction of BR's Passenger's Charter.

British Rail's Passenger's Charter: new standards for tourist rail travel?

It is widely acknowledged that BR has been perceived by passengers in the 1970s and early 1980s as an archetypal state-owned enterprise, with a negative image in relation to service provision. Although there is no simple explanation for this image, factors such as limited public funding by successive governments since the 1960s and operational difficulties (e.g. service interruptions) have contributed to the poor public perception. For example, the NCC's 'Consumer Concerns 1990' survey found that only 40 per cent of BR users were very to fairly satisfied with the service provided. This was confirmed by BR's acquisition of the Consumer Association's 'Captive Consumer Award' in January 1992 for failing to compensate consumers adequately for poor service.

BR has stated that some £7 million was paid to its customers in 1991 as cash refunds and travel vouchers through its Discretionary Compensation Scheme. However, to place service and performance on a more prominent footing, BR launched its Passenger's Charter in May 1992, with a view to having it fully operational by 1993. The funding of this new scheme was expected to cost between £10 and £15 million and it aimed to ensure that rail travel

Case study 4 (*continued*)

for tourists and commuters meets certain standards. The Charter set out to provide (British Railways Board 1992):

- a safe, punctual and reliable train service
- clean stations and clean trains
- friendly and efficient service
- clear and up to date information
- a fair and satisfactory response if things go wrong

Table 3.1 The main features of British Rail's Passenger's Charter

- Establishing performance standards and targets for groups of routes
- Setting punctuality standards
  e.g. 90 per cent of InterCity trains should arrive within 10 minutes of their scheduled time
- Setting reliability standards
  e.g. 99 per cent of InterCity services should run
- Waiting time at ticket offices should be a maximum of 5 minutes in peak periods and 3 minutes at other times
- The quality of staff communication is to be improved, particularly at retail outlets (e.g. ticket offices and enquiry bureaux) through training
- Managerial staff are to be placed on a performance-related pay scheme to ensure they reach predetermined targets
- Passengers should be kept informed prior to and during their journey of any delays
- Engineering work is to be undertaken, wherever possible, to minimise inconvenience to passengers
- Those with special needs (e.g. the disabled) are to be given assistance
- Refunds are to be made for delayed or cancelled journeys within the confines of the new compensation scheme

Source: Based on the British Railways Board (1992) *The British Rail Passenger's Charter*, London: British Railways Board.

This requires BR to establish standards for services and the most publicised aspect of the Charter was the provision of compensation for delayed or cancelled rail services. From BR's point of view, it has meant publicising its internal procedure for measuring performance. This process requires data generated through its

Case study 4 (*continued*)

Management Information Systems to monitor and evaluate different aspects of its business (Allen and Williams 1985). The main features of the Passenger's Charter are set out in Table 3.1 which shows that performance indicators and clear targets have to be met in terms of service provision. These are reviewed and published on a regular basis. In managerial terms, the process of producing the Charter may have the advantage of encouraging the development of a corporate culture based on service quality, but staff training and commitment are required if this service ethos is to permeate staff consciousness in an organisation employing over 138,000 staff.

Critics, such as the Consumers' Association, have argued that the scheme is a glossy public relations exercise with only a limited amount of finance devoted to the scheme, which may be better deployed on improving services rather than compensating travellers for poor service. Sceptics have also argued that the targets set by BR for different rail services are too low. Although it is too soon to evaluate the effectiveness of the Passenger's Charter, it is unlikely to achieve immediate results. However, it has publicised the importance of service quality and assisted BR in developing a public image as a more customer-conscious organisation. Furthermore, the Charter has provided tourists and other travellers with clearer information on their role as consumers, and the standards and attributes to expect from a rail journey. But the NCC is still seeking further improvements to the process of producing charters for public services to achieve long-term benefits for consumers (National Consumer Council 1992).

So what does the BR case study tell us about the tourist transport system?

- Marketing research is an important part of the strategic planning process for a tourist transport service, particularly when attempting to assess what the tourist and non-tourist traveller require from a rail journey. This has a critical role in establishing a benchmark for service quality to ensure minimum standards of provision are met.

- Government policy is favouring deregulation with a view to privatisation of sections of BR's network under the guise of improving consumer choice and service quality, citing the transformation in former state-owned enterprises which have been privatised and are more customer led.
- Since the 1970s, tourist use of railways in the UK has declined but there is potential for increasing the number of journeys involving air and rail, once the Channel Tunnel opens, over 500–1,000 km distances.
- Further investment is needed in the UK's aged railway rolling stock and infrastructure to improve journey times. This is likely to be limited within the context of existing policy which favours a greater role for the private sector. It is unlikely to yield major investment in new rolling stock if the franchises available to private operators are only offered on a short-term basis (e.g. 5 to 7 years).
- The introduction of the Passenger's Charter is a direct consequence of government policy towards public service provision and it has led to a greater emphasis on service quality in the tourist transport system.

Summary

It is evident from the analysis of government policy towards tourist transport that it is often subsumed under the wider remit of national transport policy-making, rather than within an integrated planning context where the relationship between transport and tourism is recognised. From this discussion of transport policy for tourism, it is evident that different political ideologies alter the continuity in investment decisions for transport planning and development which often leaves future governments with a legacy in view of the timescale involved in major tourist transport infrastructure projects coming to fruition. The influence which governments exercise on tourist transport systems to regulate the efficient movement of people cannot be viewed in a vacuum: it is not isolated from the operation, management, provision and consumption of tourist transport services. The example of the tourist rail travel system in the UK highlights this very point, emphasising the importance of a systems approach to analyse the multidisciplinary issues associated with the transport service. The situation is made more complex by the fact that the EC has also tried to influence European rail travel with its attempt to develop a Common Transport Policy.

Clearly, the situation in any tourist transport system is both dynamic and in a constant state of flux as government policy, the business environment and the requirements of the consumer are forever changing. For the innovative transport provider, staying abreast of these developments is a major challenge, although day to day operational and management issues assume so much importance in an economic activity where the logistics of moving large numbers of people from origin to destination areas for business and pleasure requires a great deal of skill and organisation. Not surprisingly, the formulation and implementation of government transport policy is often viewed as a long-term issue for any tourist transport operators as their concern for the efficient management and operation of profitable services consumes the time of operations staff. It is the corporate strategists and planners who have a long-term view of their future position in the marketplace and the means of achieving strategic planning objectives. As the Wales Tourist Board (1992: i) argue

> the provision of the basic tourism infrastructure upon which the industry depends . . . covers [the] fields of roads, public transport, information provision and visitor facilities. Accessibility from the principal visitor markets is crucial in determining the number of visitors . . . The quality of . . . facilities [and infrastructure] will undoubtedly influence the visitor's perception of Wales.

An understanding of consumer demand for tourist travel services is a fundamental requirement for tourist transport operators wishing to plan their supply services in the short to medium term. For this reason, the next chapter examines the international demand for tourist transport services and some of the data sources available to assess this issue.

Notes

1 In the Single European Act passed in June 1987, railway transport was not included.
2 The recent recession in the UK, combined with falling passenger demand, profitability and the need to be more market led, has meant that more services are only provided in response to seasonal demand, reflected in British Rail's 'Winter' and 'Summer' timetables.

Questions

1 What is the role of government policy in the regulation of the tourist transport system?
2 To what extent does EC transport policy for tourism conflict with the interests of national governments?
3 What are the underlying principles associated with British Rail's Passenger's Charter?
4 Critically assess the value of a consumer-oriented approach to tourist transport provision.

Further reading

British Railways Board (1992) *The British Rail Passenger's Charter*, London: British Railways Board. (Available from BR stations or the company's head-quarters, London.)

de Boer, E. (1986) *Transport Sociology: Social Aspects of Transport Planning*, Oxford: Pergamon.

Department of Transport (1992) *The Franchising of Passenger Rail Services: A Consultative Document*, London: Department of Transport. (Copies available from Department R, Department of Transport, Marsham Street, London.)

Halsall, D. (ed.) (1985) *Transport for Recreation*, Ormskirk: Transport Geography Study Group, Institute of British Geographers.

O'Sullivan, P. (1980) *Transport Policy: Geographic, Economic and Planning Aspects*, London: Batsford.

Vincent, M. and Green, D. (eds) (1994) *The Intercity Story*, Sparkford: Oxford Publishing Co. (esp. ch. 8, 'Delighting the customer').

The new journal *Transport Policy*, launched in 1993 and published by Butterworth-Heinemann, contains a useful range of papers on transport policy issues which have a direct and indirect bearing on tourist transport.

4
The demand for international tourist travel

Introduction

Understanding the demand for tourist transport is a critical part of the strategic planning process for transport operators and organisations associated with the management and marketing of transport services for tourists. At government level, accurate information on the use of tourist transport infrastructure is critical when formulating transport policies. Individual transport operators also need to have a clear understanding of the existing and likely patterns of demand for tourist transport, to ensure that they are able to meet the requirements of tourists. For the transport providers, high-quality market intelligence and statistical information are vital in the strategic planning process and day to day management of transport, so that the services offered are responsive and carefully targeted at demand, being both cost effective and efficient. Ultimately, transport companies seek to operate services on a commercial basis so that supply matches demand as closely as possible. The type of information required by decision-makers associated with tourist transport provision is usually gathered through the marketing research process (see Chapter 2). The type of data they require is likely to include the following:

- The geographical origin and spatial distribution of demand in the generating region.
- The demographic and socio-economic characteristics of tourist

travel demand (e.g. age, sex, family status, social class, income and expenditure).

- The geographical preferences, consumer behaviour and images of tourists for holiday destinations and tourist travel habits, including the duration of visit.
- Who is likely to organise the holiday (e.g. independently or as part of a package)?
- The choice of transport likely to be used in the tourist transport system.
- Future patterns of demand (e.g. short- and long-term forecasts of tourist travel).
- Government policy towards tourist transport operations.
- The implications of tourist travel demand for infrastructure provision and investment in tourist modes of transport (e.g. aircraft, airports, passenger liners, ferries and ports).

The purpose of this chapter is to examine the main types of data sources available to assess the international demand for tourist transport at different spatial scales, from the world scale down to individual countries. This is dealt with in the first section of the chapter, since most tourism textbooks tend to focus on definitions of tourism, tourists and ways of measuring tourism *per se*, rather than the implications of tourism statistics for assessing the demand for tourist transport. Using a case study of Tunisia, the problems in using international tourism statistics generated by the World Tourism Organisation are discussed. In the second section, a case study of international outbound tourist travel from Japan is examined to illustrate how a government's tourist travel policy to encourage a growth in demand has influenced the desire for outbound travel, and what the consequences are for tourist transport provision. In each case study, the implications for managing international and tourist transport systems are emphasised. In the last section, the need for forecasting is discussed in relation to the assessment of future demand for tourist travel, so that travel organisations (e.g. tour operators) and transport providers may plan ahead to remain competitive and anticipate tourist travel requirements.

The international demand for tourist travel

Ryan (1991) discusses the economic determinants of tourism demand which are associated with the purchase of an intangible service, usually a holiday or transport service, which comprises an experience for the tourist (see Chapter 2). The consumption of tourist transport services as part of a package holiday, or as a separate service to meet a specific need (e.g. a business trip or a visit to see friends and relatives), has manifested itself at a global scale in terms of the world-wide growth in international tourist travel. Among the economic determinants of the growth in international tourism are rising disposable incomes and increased holiday entitlement in developed countries, while transport operators have stimulated demand by more competitive pricing of air travel and other forms of travel for international tourists. This has been accompanied by the 'internationalisation' of tourism as a business activity (see Witt *et al.* 1991), as global tourism operators emerge through mergers, takeovers, strategic alliances (e.g. airlines co-operating and code sharing on routes), investment in overseas destinations and diversification into other tourism services. One consequence is that tourist transport operators view the determinants of tourist travel as crucial to their short- and long-term plans for service provision.

Aside from the economic determinants of the demand for travel, Ryan (1991) emphasises the significance of psychological determinants of demand in explaining some of the reasons why tourists travel. Although there is no theory of tourist travel, a range of tourist motivators exist (Pearce 1982). Ryan's (1991: 25–9) analysis of tourist travel motivators (excluding business travel) identifies the following reasons commonly cited to explain why people travel to tourist destinations for holidays, which include:

- a desire to escape from a mundane environment
- the pursuit of relaxation and recuperation functions
- an opportunity for play
- the strengthening of family bonds
- prestige, since different destinations can enable one to gain social enhancement among peers
- social interaction
- educational opportunities
- wish fulfilment
- shopping

Although it is possible to identify a range of motivators, it is possible to classify tourists according to the type of holiday they are seeking and the travel experience they desire. For example, Cohen (1972) distinguished between four types of tourist travellers:

- *The organised mass tourist*, on a package holiday, who is highly organised. Their contact with the host community in a destination is minimal.
- *The individual mass tourist*, who uses similar facilities to the organised mass tourist but also desires to visit other sights not covered on organised tours in the destination.
- *The explorers*, who arrange their travel independently and who wish to experience the social and cultural lifestyle of the destination.
- *The drifter*, who does not seek any contact with other tourists or their accommodation, seeking to live with the host community (see V.L. Smith 1992).

Clearly, such a classification is fraught with problems, since it does not take into account the increasing diversity of holidays undertaken and inconsistencies in tourist behaviour (Pearce 1982). Other researchers suggest that one way of overcoming this difficulty is to consider the different destinations tourists choose to visit, and then establish a sliding scale similar to Cohen's (1972) typology, but which does not have such an absolute classification. How does this affect the tourist transport system?

Both governments and transport operators need to recognise what economic, social and psychological factors are stimulating the demand for tourist travel and resulting in different types of travellers with preferences for various destinations and specific activity patterns on holiday. Tour operators selling holidays need to recognise the complexity of tourist motivation to travel and airlines need to understand the precise effect on the availability of aircraft, their ability to rotate and interchange different aircraft in a fleet to meet daily and seasonal travel requirements. For airports, the expected number of passengers, use of airspace and runways need to be planned in advance and, where there is going to be a long-term growth in demand, they may need to consider future investment and development plans. More specifically, transport operators will need to understand the range of motives and expectations of certain types of traveller since the level of service they provide will need to match the market and the requirements of travellers. Operators need to understand not only the dimensions of demand, but the market segments and the behaviour and expectations of consumers which they will need to accommodate in providing a high-quality tourist experience.

For this reason, the emphasis in this chapter is on the dimensions of international tourism demand, due to its global significance, even though in numerical terms, domestic tourism is ten times greater (Pearce 1987). A focus on international tourism will illustrate the inter-relationship between government policy and tourism demand as well as the implications for developing transport systems which both domestic and international travellers can use. However, the 'analysis [of international tourism] is complicated by the paucity of appropriate data' (Pearce 1987: 35). So, what sources of data are available to assess the demand and use of different modes of tourist transport?

Data sources

The analysis of tourism, tourists and their propensity to travel and previous travel patterns is 'a complex process . . . involving not only the visitor and his movements but also the destination and host community' (Latham 1989: 55). Tourist transport providers will often have statistical information relating to their own organisation's services and tourist use. But for a new entrant into the tourist transport business, how can they examine the feasibility of providing a transport service? What statistical information on tourist transport is available? How is it gathered? And who publishes it?

One immediate problem which confronts the researcher interested in tourist transport is the absence of international statistics which monitor every mode of tourist travel. For example, organisations such as the International Civil Aviation Organisation (ICAO) publish annual statistics on international air travel for its members' airline operations. Yet beyond industry-specific studies which monitor the volume of travel, one is forced to refer to tourism statistics since they are more comprehensive and consistent, providing an insight into:

- tourist arrivals in different regions of the world and for specific countries
- the volume of tourist trips
- types of tourism (e.g. holidaymaking, visiting friends and relatives and business travel)

- the number of nights spent in different countries by tourists
- tourist expenditure on transport-related services.

Such information may indicate the order of magnitude of tourist use of transport systems and their significance in different locations. In this context, Latham's (1989) seminal study on tourism statistics is essential reading, since it provides a useful insight into the complex process of assessing the demand for international tourist transport. Studies by Latham (1989), Jefferson and Lickorish (1991) and Veal (1992) document the procedures associated with the generation of tourism statistics, which often use social survey techniques such as questionnaire-based interviews with tourists at departure and arrival points.

Unlike other forms of social survey work, tourists are a transient and mobile population. This raises problems related to which social survey method and sampling technique one should use to generate reliable and accurate statistical information that is representative of the real world. Owing to the cost involved in undertaking social surveys, it is impossible and impractical to interview all tourists travelling on a specific mode of transport. A sampling framework is normally used to select a range of respondents who are representative of the population being examined. While there are a number of good sources which deal with this technical issue (see S.L.J. Smith 1989 and Veal 1992), it is clear that no one survey technique and sampling framework is going to provide all the information necessary to enable decision-makers to make strategic planning decisions. It is possible to discern three common types of tourism surveys:

- pre-travel studies of tourists' intended travel habits and likely use of tourist transport
- studies of tourists in transit, or at their destination, to provide information on their actual behaviour and plans for the remainder of their holiday or journey
- post-travel studies of tourists once they have returned to their place of residence.

Clearly there are advantages and disadvantages with each approach. For example, pre-travel studies may indicate the potential destinations which tourists would like to visit on their next holiday but it is difficult to assess the extent to which holiday intentions are converted to actual travel. In contrast, surveys of tourists in transit or at a destination can only provide a snapshot of their experiences to date rather than a broader evaluation of their holiday experience. Yet retrospective post-travel studies incur the problem of actually locating and eliciting responses from tourists which accurately record a previous event or experience. Each approach has a valuable role and individual transport operators and tourism organisations use the approach appropriate to their information needs.

The most comprehensive and widely used sources of tourism statistics that directly and indirectly examine international tourist travel are produced by the World Tourism Organisation (WTO) and OECD (Pearce 1987). National governments also compile statistics on international tourism for their own country (inbound travel) and the destinations chosen by outbound travellers. WTO publishes a number of annual publications including the following: the *Yearbook of Tourism Statistics* (published since 1947 as 'International Travel Statistics', then as 'World Travel Statistics', and now as 'World Travel and Tourism Statistics'). This has a summary of tourism statistics for almost 150 countries and areas with key data on tourist transport and includes statistical information in the following order:

- a world summary of international tourism statistics
- tourist arrivals
- accommodation capacity by regions
- trends in world international tourism arrivals, receipts and exports
- arrivals of cruise passengers
- domestic tourism
- tourism payments (including international tourism receipts by countries calculated in US $ millions, excluding international fare receipts)
- tourist transport (tourist arrivals from abroad by mode of transport)
- tourism motivations (arrivals from abroad and purpose of visit)
- tourism accommodation
- country studies which examine the detailed breakdown of tourism statistics collected for each area, including tourism seasonality.

In addition to WTO, OECD produces 'Tourism Policy and International Tourism in OECD Member Countries'. Although the data collected are restricted to 25 countries, it deals with other issues such as government policy and barriers to international tourism.

Table 4.1 Trends in international tourist arrivals by region, 1986–90

WTO tourist region	1986 %	1987 %	1988 %	1989 %	1990 %
Africa	3.24	3.03	3.46	3.66	3.17
The Americas	22.80	22.81	22.27	21.11	19.61
Europe	61.40	61.25	60.58	61.30	63.72
East Asia and the Pacific	8.43	8.99	9.74	10.21	10.16
South Asia	0.97	0.89	0.92	0.82	0.75
Middle East	3.13	3.00	3.00	2.88	2.56
TOTAL (000s)	330,907	356,876	382,132	415,736	443,866

Note: Totals do not add up to 100 due to rounding.

Source: Based on WTO (1992).

Recent trends in international tourism demand and tourist travel

Both WTO and OECD tourism statistics are primarily collated from national governments who supply the information according to the criteria laid down by each organisation. It is interesting to consider some of the recent trends on tourist travel and tourist transport. International tourist arrivals have risen from over 25 million in 1950 to nearly 444 million in 1990 (World Tourism Organisation 1992). Table 4.1 provides

Table 4.2 Trends in international air transport, 1986–90

	1986	1987	1988	1989	1990
World tourist arrivals (000s)	116,321	131,833	144,514	156,779	163,549
Passengers carried (000s)	197,961	221,901	243,414	265,187	261,555
Passenger kilometres (millions)	603,138	687,514	761,992	853,297	858,220

Source: Based on WTO (1992).

a breakdown of tourist arrivals by different regions of the world. The striking feature from these statistics is the continued dominance of European countries (particularly in Western Europe) as major generators of international tourist travel as well as North America. Latham (1992) explains this pattern in terms of Europe's continued dominance

Table 4.3 World's top 20 international tourism destinations in 1990

Rank 1990	Country	Tourist arrivals (000s)	Rank 1985
1	France	51,462	1
2	USA	39,772	3
3	Spain	34,300	2
4	Italy	26,679	4
5	Hungary	20,510	10
6	Austria	19,011	5
7	UK	18,021	6
8	Germany	17,045	8
9	Canada	15,258	7
10	Switzerland	13,200	9
11	China	10,484	12
12	Greece	8,873	13
13	Czechoslovakia	8,100	15
14	Portugal	8,020	14
15	Yugoslavia	7,880	11
16	Malaysia	7,477	20
17	Mexico	6,393	16
18	Hong Kong	5,933	18
19	Netherlands	5,795	19
20	Thailand	5,299	25

Source: Latham (1992: 280).

as both an origin and destination area for international tourism since its population contains segments with a high disposable income and the region has a well-developed tourism infrastructure and industry. North America, however, contains a population more inclined to take holiday trips as domestic tourists, although the sheer volume of overseas travel continues as a dominant influence. The volume of international tourist travel by air and the growth in the number of passenger kilometres travelled (see Table 4.2) also highlight the underlying growth in international travel.

When considering the distribution of global tourism flows, Hoivik and Heiberg (1980) estimated that four-fifths of all international flows were between Europe, North America and Japan and one-twentieth between other countries in the world. As Tables 4.3 and 4.4 show, in 1990 France remained the dominant tourist destination for international travel while the USA, Germany and Japan are the three most important generators of international tourism in terms of the volume of tourist expenditure. Unfortunately, in 1992 WTO did not list tourist transport statistics in their summary volume for global arrivals by air, sea and road. The only

Table 4.4 World's top 20 international tourism-generating countries by expenditure, 1990

Rank 1990	Country	Tourism expenditure (billion $US)	Rank 1980	Average annual growth rate (%) 1980–90
1	USA	38.7	2	14.1
2	Germany	30.1	1	3.9
3	Japan	24.9	6	18.4
4	UK	19.8	3	11.1
5	Italy	13.8	13	21.9
6	France	13.5	4	8.4
7	Canada	8.4	9	10.4
8	Netherlands	7.4	5	4.7
9	Austria	6.3	10	8.2
10	Switzerland	6.0	11	9.9
11	Sweden	6.0	12	10.4
12	Belgium	5.7	8	5.6
13	Mexico *	5.4	7	2.6
14	Spain	4.3	18	13.2
15	Australia	4.1	15	8.9
16	Denmark	3.7	16	9.1
17	Norway	3.4	17	10.0
18	Korea, Republic of	3.2	28	24.6
19	Finland	2.8	22	17.7
20	Singapore	1.4	29	15.9

Note: * For Mexico, the data are not strictly comparable owing to a change in methodology as from 1982.

Source: Latham (1992: 281).

Table 4.5 Cruise passenger arrivals by region in 1990

	(000s)
World	11,661
Africa	192
Americas	8,780
of which the Caribbean comprised	7,460
Asia	887
Europe	1,642
of which Southern Europe comprised	1,634
Oceania	160

Source: Based on WTO (1992).

summary provided on tourist transport was for cruise ship passenger arrivals (Table 4.5) which highlights the geographical distribution of the world cruise market which is dominated by the Caribbean and the southern Mediterranean (Peisley 1992a). For this reason, it is pertinent to consider WTO statistics for one country, Tunisia, which contain data on the different modes of transport by tourist arrivals.

Case study 5: Tourist arrivals and tourist transport in Tunisia

Tunisia is the smallest country in North Africa (Figure 4.1), with a population of 8.1 million (1990) and is an interesting example of a less developed country (LDC) which has expanded its international arrivals from 50,000 in 1962 to over 3 million in 1990 (Gant and Smith 1992). In 1990, Tunisia was the world's 27th most popular international tourism destination (WTO 1992). Gant and Smith (1992) examine the problems of using WTO statistics to gauge the scale of tourist arrivals. The inclusion of periodic influxes of nomadic people (non-tourists) from other neighbouring Arab countries means that they considered tourist nights in residence, which gives a clearer indication of demand. However, in terms of tourist transport, WTO's arrival data illustrate who is travelling to Tunisia and the implications for the provision and use of transport infrastructure. They also indicate the importance of transport infrastructure and its potential in utilising the country's diverse tourism resources to diversify the tourism product. Table 4.6 shows that the non-tourist arrivals by road from North Africa distort the real pattern, but it does show Tunisia's importance as a port of call for cruise ships. By cross-checking WTO's cruise passenger arrival statistics and the Tunisia country profile, one finds that 45,000 of the 64,676 arrivals by sea in 1990 were cruise ship passengers, mainly from Western Europe, particularly France and Germany, with Tunis the main entry point (gateway). The majority of international tourist arrivals were by air and reached nearly 2 million in 1990. Gant and Smith (1992) calculate that Germany, France and the UK were the dominant source areas and WTO figures (see Table 4.6 – second column) show that 1.1 million of arrivals were from Western Europe, with the French

Case study 5 (*continued*)

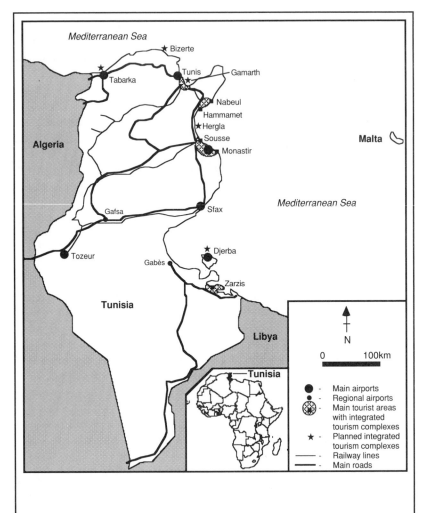

Figure 4.1 The tourist transport system in Tunisia

Case study 5 (*continued*)

Table 4.6 International tourist arrivals in Tunisia by mode of transport in 1990

	By air	%	By road	%	By sea	%
AFRICA	91,166	4.98	1,278,343	97.68	17,205	26.60
Algeria	42,466	2.31	389,229	29.74	3,514	5.43
Libya	23,925	1.30	771,154	58.93	713	1.10
Morocco	16,024	0.87	115,173	8.80	12,753	19.71
Other Africa	8,751	0.47	2,787	0.21	225	0.34
AMERICAS	11,528	0.62	444	0.3	627	0.96
USA	8,264	0.45	145	0.1	478	0.73
Canada	3,264	0.17	299	0.2	149	0.23
ASIA	32,476	1.77	12,908	0.98	347	0.53
EUROPE	1,647,311	89.99	13,432	1.02	44,708	69.12
UK	190,330	16.39	396	0.03	637	0.98
Scandinavia	76,303	4.16	313	0.02	490	0.75
Italy	174,217	9.51	2,513	0.19	12,732	19.68
Spain	32,917	1.79	311	0.02	430	0.66
Yugoslavia	13,155	0.71	336	0.02	331	0.51
Austria	36,261	1.98	606	0.04	1,734	2.68
Belgium	73,096	3.99	168	0.01	1,098	1.69
France	439,343	24	4,085	0.31	14,694	22.71
Germany	466,414	25.47	3,795	0.29	9,214	14.24
Luxembourg	4,539	0.24	2	–	12	0.01
Netherlands	95,887	5.23	190	0.01	682	1.05
Switzerland	44,849	2.45	717	0.05	2,654	4.10
OTHER AREAS	48,042	2.62	3,452	0.26	1,789	2.76
TOTAL	1,781,077	100	1,308,579	100	64,676	100

Source: Based on WTO (1992).

(24 per cent), German (25.4 per cent), UK (16.39 per cent) and Italian tourists (9.51 per cent) dominating the pattern, many on inclusive-tour beach-holidays, with 75 per cent concentrated in the period April to October (Gant and Smith 1992). In terms of tourism development, this has resulted in a geographical concentration of mass tourism along Tunisia's coastline in integrated tourism complexes (Figure 4.1). Some five international-standard airports have been developed to accommodate this growth in international tourism (Figure 4.1). However, providing opportunities to travel into the Sahara and the unique experience of an arid

Case study 5 (*continued*)

environment has been dependent upon state investment in the upgrading of Tozeur airport to international standard and improved road access (Figure 4.1). The first flights to Tozeur airport from Paris commenced in 1990, which enabled it to develop as a centre for four-wheeled-vehicle excursions into the Sahara. Investment by a hotel chain, to accommodate tourists along this new trail across southern Tunisia, has added to the tourism infrastructure to develop this tourist trail through the Sahara (Gant and Smith 1992).

Clearly, the development of Tunisia's international tourism industry has provided many opportunities for tour operators to develop new tourism products related to developments in the tourist transport system. A sound understanding of tourism trends in WTO sources and OECD publications is an important starting point for the analysis of international tourism demand. WTO statistics on tourism provide an essential baseline of data for transport providers so that more detailed market research (e.g. holiday intentions surveys) can be commissioned to assess specific aspects of tourist travel requirements for individual destinations and for internal travel within the host country. The Tunisian case study provides an insight into the significance of tourism in an LDC and the significance of efficient and quality tourist transport systems, an issue developed in Chapter 5. Pearce (1990) and Lickorish *et al.* (1991) argue that an inadequate transport infrastructure may actually constrain the development of international tourism in LDCs. Yet the case of Tunisia suggests that a sound understanding of international tourism demand by the government and private sector transport operators has enabled the country to develop a tourism economy where tourist travel services make a significant contribution to the balance of payments.

Other statistical sources on international tourist travel

At a transnational level, the EC is also an important source of statistical information on tourist transport (Jefferson and Lickorish 1991). The EC has undertaken various studies of tourist travel, most notably the 1986 Omnibus Survey *The Europeans and their Holidays* which examined the travel patterns in member states and recognises the overwhelming importance of car-borne travel. Although Table 4.7 is dated, it remains one of the comprehensive sources of data on tourist modes of travel between member states. More recently, the EC publication *Transport, Communications, Tourism Statistical Yearbook* (Eurostat 1987) recorded generalised time series statistics on tourist travel in relation to:

Table 4.7 Mode of transport used by European holidaymakers

	Car %	Train %	Plane %	Boat %	Bike %/ Motorbike %	Coach %
By origin						
Belgium	77	6	10	1	8	7
Denmark	59	14	18	11	3	4
France	81	15	6	2	2	7
Germany	61	16	17	3	1	7
Greece	78	4	13	25	1	0
Ireland	51	11	31	18	1	6
Italy	73	15	5	5	2	11
Luxembourg	62	10	19	4	0	15
Netherlands	70	8	14	5	6	14
Portugal	76	17	3	3	1	16
Spain	70	16	5	2	0	12
United Kingdom	59	11	24	8	0	14
EC Member States	68	14	13	5	1	10
By destination						
Own country	78	14	1	8	1	8
Other country	52	11	32	6	2	13
Non-EC Europe	53	15	29	17	0	18
Outside Europe	35	19	86	1	0	15

Note: Totals exceed 100 owing to multiple responses.

Source: EC Omnibus Survey, cited in Page (1993d: 12).

- transport infrastructure in member states
- distances covered by various modes of transport
- definitions and explanations of tourist travel on railways, roads, waterways and aircraft by country
- summary information on tourism demand.

It is evident from Eurostat sources that there is a high level of intra-regional tourist travel (i.e. international tourist travel within the EC).

For example, in 1989 there were 220,779,000 tourist trips in the Europe/ Mediterranean region, the majority undertaken by West German (25.5 per cent), French (9.5 per cent), UK (9 per cent), Dutch (5.4 per cent), Swiss (5.3 per cent) and Italian (4.9 per cent) tourists (Page 1993d). For these trips, air and road travel assumes an important role. For more detailed analyses of tourist use of transport systems, EC data can be complemented by international travel surveys undertaken by member states. These are well documented in accessible sources such as Latham (1989) and Jefferson and Lickorish (1991) and the technical issues associated with these surveys need not be reiterated here. In the UK, the most important government survey of international tourist travel is the International Passenger Survey (IPS) which began in 1961 and is a stratified random sample of tourists arriving/departing from the UK's main ports of entry. Latham (1989: 64) identifies its principal aims as the collection of:

- data on the government's travel account (expenditure by incoming tourists and outgoing visitors) which are used to calculate tourism's contribution
- detailed information on visitors to the UK and outbound travellers to overseas destinations
- information on international migration
- data on the routes used by tourists to assist shipping and aviation authorities.

These statistics are published annually in a revised format as International Passenger Transport (HMSO 1990), although for a commercial annual subscription (now in excess of £20,000), companies can purchase the raw data from the IPS survey and additional questions can be added to the survey at a cost to transport operators. In addition, organisations such as the UK's Civil Aviation Authority publish quarterly summaries of air transport statistics to and from the UK and the Department of Transport produces the UK Transport Statistics, although they do not distinguish between tourist and non-tourist use of transport. *Ad hoc* studies, such as the UK Long Distance Travel Survey (see Chapter 3), also provide more detailed insights into the use of tourist transport. Although few tourism surveys specifically target tourist transport as the primary focus, there are sources of data generated by these studies which can be used to understand the nature of international tourist use of different forms of transport.

From this discussion of data sources on international tourism demand, it should be evident that up to date market intelligence is essential for tourist transport operators, particularly in a situation where demand is increasing at a rapid rate. For this reason, attention now turns to a case study of outbound travel from Japan.

Case study 6: The demand for outbound tourist travel and the transport system in Japan

One of the main areas of expansion in outbound travel in the 1980s was the Pacific Rim, which comprises the established industrial and newly industrialised countries of South East Asia, most notably Japan (Edwards 1992). The continued growth in outbound travel from these markets has attracted a great deal of interest from the tourist transport operators, especially global airlines, since these markets have been growing at a time of relative stagnation in many of the mature outbound travel markets in North America and Western Europe. Japan (Figure 4.2) is an interesting example as it was the third largest generator of international tourism expenditure in 1990, after North America and Germany. It is a lucrative market which many international tourist destinations have nurtured, given that its 123 million population comprises an emergent market for international tourism. According to Nozawa (1992), Japanese travel to destinations in the Pacific Asia regions (i.e. Australia and New Zealand) is set to expand, while Canada and Switzerland are other popular long-haul destinations (see Page 1989a for a discussion of Japanese outbound travel to New Zealand). Within Western Europe, the UK, France and Italy were also 'desirable destinations for historical . . . sightseeing and folklore tours' for Japanese tourists (Nozawa 1992: 232) and in the Pacific Asia region, destinations such as Thailand, Singapore and Hong Kong have remained popular (Morris 1990). This case study examines the situation in Japan in the 1980s and 1990s and the significance of a positive government policy designed to expand outbound tourist travel. Emphasis is placed on the factors associated with a boom in outbound travel and the constraints imposed by the existing tourist transport system which is inhibiting further growth. This is followed by a discussion of the prospects for the 1990s. It is pertinent, however, to commence with a discussion of

Case study 6 (*continued*)

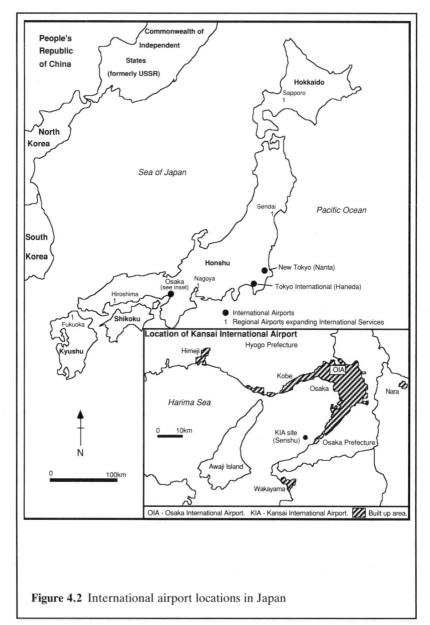

Figure 4.2 International airport locations in Japan

Case study 6 (*continued*)

sources of data on international tourism demand in Japan and the historical evolution of outbound travel to place the case study in a broader context.

Data sources on Japanese outbound travel

According to Pearce (1987), one of the main sources of data available to assess international travel by Japanese tourists is the passport applications generated by the Ministry of Justice's Immigration Bureau prior to 1970. Since there were restrictions on outbound travel from Japan prior to 1970, these data provide evidence of the 'purpose of visit and main country visited' (Pearce 1987). After 1970, restrictions on travel and multiple visa applications were gradually lifted making the data more difficult to analyse, and therefore recent trends are calculated using a number of statistical sources. The Ministry of Justice still collates passport applications, but the Japanese National Tourist Organisation reanalyses the data to ensure they are consistent with the methodology employed by organisations such as WTO. In addition, the Ministry of Transport, whose responsibility is the formulation and implementation of tourism policy, collects tourism data for policy purposes.

The evolution of tourism demand

Pearce (1987) documents the evolution of Japanese outbound travel between 1964 and 1981, where the number of tourists travelling increased from 100,000 to over 4 million (Tokuhisa 1980). A number of factors can be attributed to this rapid expansion in demand:

- a continued growth in international trade and the generation of wealth from activities in the Japanese economy
- increased personal affluence for the population and additional disposable income to spend on luxury items like travel
- the liberalisation of currency restrictions in 1964

Case study 6 (*continued*)

- the easing of administrative procedures to obtain a passport and visa
- improved aircraft technology which facilitated easier access to overseas destinations
- the development and marketing of package holidays which reduced the price of travel.

Since 1981, outbound tourist travel has expanded at an ever greater rate than the 1970s, with the number of outbound trips more than doubling from 5 to 11 million between 1986 and 1991. This growth has caused a great deal of debate among analysts over the extent to which it was stimulated by government policy as opposed to resulting from an underlying trend towards international travel in Japanese society. For example, Polunin (1989) interprets this expansion as a result of an underlying growth within Japanese society which was only marginally influenced by official policy. The significance of Polunin's (1989) analysis is that whilst encouraging a growth in demand, the government has failed to match this with an expansion in the supply of tourist transport infrastructure to accommodate growth. For this reason, it is useful to examine the role of government policy in stimulating the demand for outbound travel, followed by the range of underlying factors which both Polunin (1989) and Nozawa (1992) cite as influential in shaping demand.

Government policy and outbound travel in Japan

In 1986, the Japanese government announced its 'Ten Million Programme' which sought to encourage a doubling of outbound travel between 1986 and 1991. The rationale for this programme has been interpreted in various ways, including:

- the promotion of international citizenship among its population
- a response to growing international pressure for Japan to reduce its trade surplus generated through its balance of payments, and
- a strong export-led economy in the 1970s and 1980s.

Case study 6 (*continued*)

Polunin (1989) suggests that this policy was little more than a public relations exercise since outbound travel was already expanding by over 11 per cent in 1986 and this trend continued with expansion in excess of 20 per cent in 1987 and 1988. However, the significance of this policy statement was that the 'Japanese tend to regard government bureaucrats as well-intentioned partners in progress. . . . They respond positively to being told what to do. The Ten Million Programme says that travel is desirable and indeed expected' (Polunin 1989: 6). In this context, the Ten Million Programme may be viewed as legitimising outbound travel in Japanese society, as there are cultural barriers to travel, since the work ethic has traditionally negated against long holidays. Government policy endorsed outbound travel and positively encouraged travel as a way of addressing international criticism of the accumulating trade surplus.

More recently, the government's Ten Million Programme has been expanded to incorporate the 'Two Way Tourism 21 Programme', designed to nurture incoming tourism to Japan. This has focused on attracting the growing Asian outbound markets, based on the unique culture, history and traditions of Japanese society. This policy aimed to boost the existing $3,435 million receipts from inbound tourists in 1991 to offset the $23,983 million spent by outbound Japanese travellers. Yet for the tourist transport operators in Japan it is interesting to ascertain what factors have facilitated the Japanese 'travel boom' in the late 1980s and the effect of expansion in demand for the tourist transport system.

What factors facilitated an expansion of outbound travel from Japan in the 1980s?

Polunin (1989) argues that the growing internationalism of Japanese society has encouraged a growth in outbound tourism, as Japan developed a more outward-looking position in the world economy accompanied by increased international investment in overseas countries. Such a change in outlook led to an increased awareness in Japanese society of the desirability of overseas travel.

Case study 6 (*continued*)

Nozawa (1992) argues that the 1989 annual White Paper on Leisure Activity in Japan found that 32 per cent of respondents would like to travel abroad if given an extra day off a week. This reflects a shift in emphasis within Japanese society from the work ethic, as in '1987 average annual Japanese working hours were 2150 hours compared with typical US hours of 1924' (Nozawa 1992: 228). Hard work and loyalty to one's company have traditionally resulted in long working hours and few official overseas holidays. However, a number of specific factors appear to have stimulated a Japanese 'travel boom' in the 1980s:

- Japan's gross national product outperformed the world average in the 1980s creating additional disposable income available for discretionary spending on tourism and leisure services in Japan.
- In 1986, the state ended Japan Airline's (JAL) monopoly of international scheduled services (Polunin 1989) and some of the capacity constraints of the late 1970s; the 1980s were characterised by additional airlines offering extra scheduled services. In 1991, there were 52 scheduled airlines operating to 32 destinations and a further 43 seeking traffic rights.
- In 1987, the International Tourism Institute of Japan was formed to assist the government in the promotion of outbound travel, providing tourism consultants to developing countries on projects assigned by the Ministry of Transport (Nozawa 1992).
- The Japanese government encouraged the Ministry of Labour to reduce the working week from 48 to 40 hours a week in 1988 to generate additional leisure time for overseas travel. It was followed by the promotion of a 'Long Holiday Week' and a 'Tourism Week' to encourage outbound rather than domestic travel.
- The year of 1988 was deemed 'the year of liberalization for Japanese tourism' (Nozawa 1992: 227), with a streamlining of emigration procedures and tax privileges for outbound travel (see Morris 1990).
- The Japanese government has negotiated bilateral visa waivers for short-stay visitors in other countries, most notably the USA

Case study 6 (*continued*)

in 1988, which stimulated an increase in demand for visits to this destination.

- Overseas investment by Japanese tourist transport enterprises has been characterised by the diversification into overseas hotels (Morris 1990), as Japan's international carriers (e.g. JAL and All Nippon Airways) secured a stake in the major destinations served by these airlines (see Go and Murakami 1990). For example, Morris (1990) notes that 60 per cent of hotel rooms in Hawaii are owned by Japanese companies.
- A 'Working Holiday Scheme' for young Japanese travellers was developed for Australia and subsequently expanded to New Zealand and Canada.
- State investment in international airports and the promotion of regional airports for the use of charter flights on inclusive tours has only had a marginal impact on capacity constraints at Narita and Osaka international airports.

Unfortunately, the demand for outbound travel and its continued expansion in the late 1980s and early 1990s has not been matched by the supply of airport capacity. One simple explanation is that airport development requires a long-term programme which is phased in over a number of years (see Doganis 1992). The expansion in demand of over 20 per cent per annum in the late 1980s would be difficult to accommodate in any tourist transport system. Hunt (1988) notes that a Bank of Japan study on Japanese airports found 1.5 million tourist trips were deterred by capacity constraints (e.g. Narita and Itami airports only have one runway). According to Nozawa (1992) this was compounded by a curfew on night flying, constraining existing capacity by 30 per cent. In addition, the expansion of Narita airport (see Figure 4.2) with two extra runways and a new terminal has been delayed until 1995. Among Japan's regional airports which operate as international gateways, an absence of long runways, terminal facilities and associated services has constrained expansion. In Osaka (see Figure 4.2) an innovative solution to the problem has been the construction of the new Kansai International Airport on a floating island.

Case study 6 (*continued*)

Kansai International Airport

Therivel and Barrett (1990) examine the construction of this new airport, focusing on the environmental impact of developing a 24 hour service in a country where land is a scarce commodity. Kansai International Airport (KIA) is located in central Japan (Figure 4.2), and will provide much needed access to Asia (Morris 1990). KIA was conceived to avoid the complaints and problems associated with Osaka International Airport, which was built near a densely populated area and attracted considerable public criticism due to noise pollution (see Chapter 6). The planning of KIA can be dated back to the 1960s. Based on a feasibility study of sites in 1968, an Aviation Deliberation Council (ADC) examined seven sites in the Osaka region, with a view to being able to (Therivel and Barrett 1990: 82):

- handle domestic and international flights
- offer 24 hour airport operation
- provide comprehensive environmental protection
- offer the possibility of further expansion,

It was not until 1974 that the Japanese Ministry of Transport released the ADC report and this identified a site 5 km off Senshu as the preferred location (Figure 4.2). Despite opposition from the local authorities concerning the environmental impact of such a project, a decline in the local economy in the mid-1970s prompted a greater consideration of local planning gains from the project (Therivel and Barrett 1990). In 1982, following environmental reports, the project was approved and the KIA Company was formed. The Company's plans sought (Therivel and Barrett 1990: 83):

- 511 ha of reclaimed land
- a 3,500 m runway
- terminals and associated buildings
- capacity for 160,000 take-offs and landings per annum
- a second phase to expand the site by 1200 ha with two additional runways of 3,000 m and 3,500 m.

Case study 6 (*continued*)

The airport received planning permission after a complex environmental review process (see Chapter 6 for a more detailed
discussion of environmental assessment) and opened in 1994,
15 months behind schedule owing to landfill problems associated
with reclamation works. This has meant that the project is over
budget at Y1.4 trillion which may jeopardise the second-phase
expansion owing to the estimated Y1.8 trillion cost. But what are
the prospects for improving international airport capacity in other
regions of Japan in the 1990s?

The Ministry of Transport's 'Five Year Airport Development
Plan' (1991–5) advocated that a further Y3.19 trillion was needed
for investment in airport infrastructure. However, almost 60 per
cent of the budget has already been allocated to projects at Narita,
Haneda and KIA and the upgrading of regional airports (see
Figure 4.2).

Lessons from the Japanese experience

- Facilitating an expansion in the demand for outbound travel
  requires appropriate investment in tourist transport infrastructure so that inadequate supply does not constrain
  demand.
- The rhetoric and actions of government policy need to be set in
  a rational framework where the demand for outbound travel is
  sensitively managed to avoid congestion and a decline in the
  quality of the 'tourists' travel experience'. Deregulating and
  liberalising air travel in Japan was not a short-term solution to
  expanding capacity, as airports are seriously constrained in
  terms of the volume of traffic they can accommodate.
- Measures to facilitate outbound travel need to be phased in as
  new airport capacity comes on stream.
- The lead time and cost of airport investment has meant that an
  expansion in outbound travel could not be achieved in the
  timespan of the 5 years envisaged in the 'Ten Million
  Programme'. This has added to existing congestion and
  deterred potential Japanese tourists from travelling.

Case study 6 (*continued*)

Prospects for the Japanese outbound market in the 1990s: implications for tourist transport systems

It is evident from the number of operators seeking to develop airline operations to serve Japan and the Pacific Rim that the Japanese outbound market offers considerable potential for the 1990s. Morris (1990) forecast that the outbound market would double by the year 2000, reaching 20 million trips, averaging annual growth rates of approximately 10 per cent. Nozawa (1992) finds that market research in Japan suggests outbound travel would expand in the following market segments:

- outbound travel by the female traveller market would grow, especially in the 20–39 age group among office professionals (single females with a high discretionary income)
- Japanese housewives using package tours
- older married couples aged 45 or more ('Full Mooners')
- the 'Silver Market' (the over 60s)

markets which were discussed by Page (1989a) within the context of New Zealand.

Outbound Japanese tourists are likely to require more sophisticated package tours and independent travel on scheduled airlines. Since the Japanese tourist is preoccupied with quality in service provision, airlines and providers of tourism services will need to be conscious of the needs and 'tourist experience' sought by these travellers. Repeat travel among the Japanese to destinations they visited on package tours is growing, particularly in New Zealand, as sightseeing and touring dominate their itineraries, offering potential niche markets for transport service providers in destination areas. The tendency for shorter stays abroad and the complex motives among Japanese tourists remain important, which tour operators and tourist transport systems must try to understand if they are to nurture the Japanese market (Morean 1983; Moore 1985). Understanding the objectives and values of such travellers (e.g. the desire for service quality and safety) will affect the perception and image of specific tourist transport systems in the

Case study 6 (*continued*)

1990s and the airlines they choose to fly on. Transport operators serving Japan need to recognise not only the dimensions of demand in inbound and outbound tourism markets, but also how future demand will be accommodated in tourist transport systems. The Japanese case study shows that infrastructure was unable to balance the demand with adequate supply. Therefore, attention now turns to the significance of tourism forecasting in understanding future patterns of tourist demand for travel, since a sophisticated analysis of this issue may enable transport planners and policy-makers to recognise the opportunities for tourist transport systems from the provision of adequate infrastructure to meet demand.

Forecasting the demand for tourist transport

According to Jefferson and Lickorish (1991: 101), forecasting the demand for tourist transport is essential for commercial operators, 'whether in the public or private sector . . . [as they] . . . will seek to maximise revenue and profits in moving towards maximum efficiency in [their] use of resources'. Archer (1987) argues that:

no manager can avoid the need for some form of forecasting: a manager must plan for the future in order to minimise the risk of failure or, more optimistically, to maximise the possibilities of success. In order to plan, he must use forecasts. Forecasts will always be made, whether by guesswork, teamwork or the use of complex models, and the accuracy of the forecasts will affect the quality of the management decision.

(Archer 1987: 77)

Reliable forecasts are essential for managers and decision-makers involved in service provision within the tourist transport system to try and ensure adequate supply is available to meet demand, while ensuring oversupply does not result, since this can erode the profitability of their operation. In essence, 'forecasts of tourism demand are essential for efficient planning by airlines, shipping companies, railways, coach operators, hoteliers [*sic*], tour operators' (Witt *et al.* 1991: 52).

Forecasting is the process associated with an assessment of future changes in the demand for tourist transport. It must be stressed that 'forecasting is not an exact science' (Jefferson and Lickorish 1991: 102), as it attempts to make estimations of future traffic potential and a range of possible scenarios, which provide an indication of the likely scale of change in demand. Consequently, forecasting is a technique used to suggest the future pattern of demand, thereby requiring associated marketing activity to exploit the market for tourist transport services.

According to Jefferson and Lickorish (1991: 102) the principal methods of forecasting are:

- 'the projection by extrapolation, of historic trends' (i.e. how the previous performance of demand may shape future patterns)
- 'extrapolation, subject to the application of . . . [statistical analysis using] . . . weights or variables'

In addition,

- structured group discussions among a panel of tourism–transport experts may be used to assess factors determining future traffic forecasts ('The Delphi Method').

Bull (1991) recognises that the range of tourism forecasting techniques is determined by the methods of analysis they employ. There are two basic types of forecasting method:

- those based on qualitative techniques, such as the Delphi method. Archer (1987) argues that these are viewed considerably less rigorously than
- quantitative forecasting methods, using techniques developed from statistics and economic theory.

Bull (1991: 127–8) classifies the quantitative techniques forecasters use in terms of the degree of statistical and mathematical complexity based on:

- time series analysis of trends (e.g. seasonality in travel) which involves simple statistical calculations to consider how past trends may be replicated in the future
- economic-theory-based models, used in econometrics (see Witt and Martin 1992).

Clearly, in an introductory book such as this, there is insufficient space to consider the detailed technical aspects of forecasting which are reviewed in a number of other good sources (e.g. Archer 1987; Witt and Martin 1992). The important issue to recognise here is that in forecasting, a number of variables are examined which relate to factors directly and indirectly influencing tourist travel. These variables are considered according to their statistical relationship with each other. Bull (1991: 127) notes that the most common variables used are:

- number of tourist trips
- total tourist expenditure and expenditure per capita
- market shares of tourism
- the tourism sector's share of gross domestic product.

Depending on the complexity of the methodology employed, the forecasting model may examine one dependent variable (e.g. tourist trips) and how other independent variables (e.g. the state of the national and international economy, leisure time, levels of disposable income, inflation and foreign exchange rates) affect the demand for tourist trips.

Approaches to forecasting can also be classified according to what they are attempting to do. For example, time series models of tourism using statistical techniques such as 'moving averages' (see Witt and Martin 1989: 6) may be easy and relatively inexpensive to undertake, but they are 'non-causal'. This means that they do not explain what specific factors are shaping the trends: they only indicate what is happening in terms of observed trends. In fact, there is also evidence that non-causal techniques have been more accurate than more complex econometric models (Witt *et al.* 1991). Econometric models are termed 'causal' since they are searching for statistical relationships to suggest what is causing tourist trips to take a certain form, thereby producing particular trends. Thus, the level of complexity involved in causal modelling is considerably greater.

Usyal and Crompton (1985) provide a good overview of different methods used to forecast tourism demand, concluding that:

Qualitative approaches when combined with quantitative approaches enable forecasts to be amended to incorporate relevant consumer demand data. When used alone quantitative models have conceptual limitations. Typically they are philosophically blind. . . . Lack of appropriate data means that they are unable to incorporate an understanding of consumer motivations and behaviour which explain tourism demand and may cause it to shift unpredictably in the future.

(Usyal and Crompton 1985: 14)

Ultimately, forecasting attempts to establish how consumer demand for tourist transport has shaped previous trends and how these may change in the future, often over a 5 to 10 year period. At a world scale, the detailed study by Edwards (1992) *Long Term Tourism Forecasts to 2005* is a useful source to examine in trying to assess how the demand for tourist transport will change on a global basis and within different countries over the next decade. A useful discussion of the significance of using forecasts of tourist use of a new transport system can be found in Page and Sinclair's (1992b) analysis of the demand for Channel Tunnel rail services.

Summary

This chapter has shown that the demand for tourist transport can be examined from a range of accessible data sources published by the WTO and OECD which may be complemented by more detailed research by individual transport operators interested in understanding the needs of their customers. As both Chapter 3 and this chapter emphasised, the demand for tourist transport can be directly influenced by government policy to expand both incoming tourism (e.g. Tunisia) and outbound tourism (e.g. Japan), although this has important consequences for infrastructure provision and the supply of tourist transport which is dealt with in the next chapter. In the case of Tunisia, the government has assisted the private sector tourism industry by supporting the diversification from mass tourism focused on integrated tourism complexes in coastal areas into niche markets in inland resorts. Government-funded transport projects and associated infrastructure provision (i.e. hotel projects) have assisted in the realisation of new tourism opportunities based on the land-based transport system (e.g. four-wheel-drive tours into the Sahara desert).

In contrast, the 'Ten Million Programme' promoted by the Japanese government appeared to overlook the constraints imposed by airport capacity, despite the licensing of new carriers and routes to serve the Japanese market. As an emerging market for outbound tourism, many airline companies have set their sights on penetrating this market in the

1990s at a time of relative stagnation in other mature travel markets. Such strategies are based on forecasts of the likely growth in the Japanese outbound market since companies need to establish how future investment programmes in new routes and infrastructure can be justified. It is not surprising that large tourist transport operators employ forecasting experts in-house and use a variety of transport analysts to ensure that they receive the best sources of market intelligence to remain competitive. Such information inevitably remains confidential, even though forecasting is not an exact science which is able to offer definitive answers on how particular tourist markets will perform over a 5 to 10 year timespan. Yet the demand for tourist transport should not be viewed in isolation from supply issues. The tourist transport system operates through the interplay of government policy, consumer demand and the supply of transport services. For this reason, the next chapter considers the supply of tourist transport services.

Questions

1 What are the main published sources of data available to researchers interested in tourist transport?
2 What are the main transport-related problems associated with the expansion of Japan's outbound tourism market?
3 Why do tourist transport organisations undertake forecasting?
4 What are the main types of forecasting technique which researchers use when assessing the future market potential for tourist transport services?

Further reading

Archer, B.H. (1987) 'Demand forecasting and estimation', in J.R.B. Ritchie and C.R. Goeldner (eds) *Travel, Tourism and Hospitality Research: A Handbook for Managers and Researchers*, New York: Wiley: 77–85.
Krippendorf, J. (1991) *The Holiday Makers: Understanding the Impact of Leisure and Travel*, London: Butterworth-Heinemann.
Morris, S. (1994) 'Japan outbound', *Travel and Tourism Analyst* 1: 40–64.
Pitfield, D.E. (1993) 'Predicting air transport demand', *Environment and Planning A* 25, 4: 459–66.
Withyman, W. (1985) 'The ins and outs of international travel and tourism data', *International Tourism Quarterly* Special Report No. 55.
Witt, S. and Martin, C. (1992) *Modelling and Forecasting Demand in Tourism*, London: Academic Press.

5
The supply of transport
for tourists

Introduction

In Chapter 2 the concept of supply was discussed in relation to the analysis of transport and tourism. In contrast to demand issues (Chapter 4), there is a relative paucity of research on supply issues in tourism and transport studies (Eadington and Redman 1991). Witt *et al.* (1991) consider that one of the main reasons for this absence is that the:

> subset of transport studies that directly relates to tourism is relatively neglected . . . [and] . . . it is a major task of research to bring together the work done in transport studies with that more special-ised work on tourism . . . [as] . . . many of the relevant studies are privately commissioned and often not widely disseminated.
>
> (Witt *et al.* 1991: 155–6)

The absence of any synthesis of supply-related research which integrates tourism and transport into a more cohesive framework led Sinclair (1991: 6) to argue that the 'literature on transportation and its impli-cations for domestic and international tourism merits separate analysis'. The efficient management and operation of transport systems for tour-ists requires that demand issues are analysed in relation to supply since the two issues co-exist and they determine the future pattern of use and activities within the tourist transport system.

The supply of tourist transport has been dealt with in various popular tourism textbooks familiar to many readers (e.g. Holloway 1989; Lavery

1989), which consider the characteristics, principles and organisation associated with each mode of tourist transport. In an introductory book such as this, it is inappropriate to reiterate the empirical discussion of different modes of transport in these publications. Furthermore, a variety of good accessible publications also document many of the issues associated with different modes of tourist transport using up to date market intelligence compiled by transport analysts (Economist Intelligence publications such as *Travel and Tourism Analyst* and their Occasional Reports). For this reason, this chapter considers some of the broader issues affecting the supply of tourist transport and introduces a number of different ways of researching and analysing supply issues. The chapter develops a framework in which both the traveller and transport provider's perspectives are considered in relation to an underlying concern for service quality. The concept of transaction analysis is introduced as a method of understanding the central role of transport in the supply of tourist travel. Transaction analysis assists in assessing the transport supplier's involvement in the distribution chain and the ways in which they may influence and control the chain and service quality in the supply of transport services. To illustrate the extent of one transport operator's involvement in the distribution chain, a case study of Singapore International Airlines is examined.

Understanding the supply chain in tourist transport services

The absence of detailed research on the supply of tourism and transport services has been a major constraint on the development of literature in this area. The situation has been compounded by the image of supply research in tourism and transport studies which is sometimes perceived as descriptive, lacking intellectual rigour and sophisticated methods of study, since 'generally there is little research on the tourism [and transport] industry and its operation which is analytical in emphasis' (Sinclair and Stabler 1991: 2). This is perpetuated by the treatment of supply issues in many general tourism texts which broadly discuss 'passenger transportation' since there are methodological problems in differentiating between the supply and use of transport services by the local population for travel to work, leisure and recreational travel purposes and more specifically for tourist use. Thus it is not surprising to find that research has focused on established areas of tourism and transport supply, notably (Sinclair and Stabler 1991: 2):

- descriptions of the industry and its operation, management and marketing
- the spatial development and interactions which characterise the industry at different geographical scales.

Studies of transport systems within tourism research have been characterised by a preoccupation with how their operations are organised to provide a service to travellers and the international nature of transportation to facilitate tourism activities and development. This approach to research on tourist transport systems is rooted in economics, as emphasised in Chapter 2, based on the concept of the 'firm' developed by Coase (1937) and discussed further by Buckley and Casson (1985). In the context of tourism and transport supply, Buckley (1987) notes that the analysis of a firm or company is characterised by certain relationships within the organisation and with its purchasers or consumers. The external process of selling a product or service involves a transaction between two parties following an agreement to purchase often, though not exclusively, involving a monetary transaction. Commercial transactions are based on agreed conditions and enforced within a framework of contractual obligations between each party. Therefore, transaction chains develop to link the tourist with the suppliers of services in tourism and the 'tourism product or service' is defined as the sum of these transactions (Witt *et al.* 1991: 81). Such research highlights the significance of the 'chain of distribution' for transport and tourism services, which is the method of distribution of the service from the production through to the eventual consumption by tourists. A more general discussion of the distribution chain in tourism can be found in Holloway (1989: 54–5).

Transaction analysis

Buckley (1987) describes some typical transaction chains for tourism which identify the integral role of transport services in linking origin and destination areas (see Figure 5.1). The nature of the specific supply chain depends upon a wide range of factors which are internal and external to individual firms in the transport sector. For example, what is the primary force driving the supply system? Is it driven by pull factors, where a tourist destination may market a region and supply transport services on a state-owned airline to stimulate demand for tourism? Or is it driven by push factors, where the tourist generates the demand, and the transport and accommodation sectors respond to this as a commercial opportunity? The overall business environment, government predisposition to tourism and planning constraints may have a moderating influence on the supply system. In addition, transaction analysis illustrates the significance of 'agents' in the system, corporate policy in transport provision and contractual arrangements in the supply chain.

Much of the existing knowledge available on these issues has been generated through interviews with managers in each sector of the transport industry and their commercial practices (e.g. contracting arrangements, profit margins and global strategies). It is rare to find researchers being given access to commercial information on supply (and demand) issues, owing to the confidential and sensitive nature of the data, and the perceived threat it may pose to their competitive advantage if rival operators obtained such information. In some cases this amounts to paranoia among companies, as media coverage of the British Airways and Virgin Atlantic libel case in 1992–3 highlighted. The result is that the relationship between transport supply and tourist use remains poorly understood with commercial research primarily concerned with the effect of pricing transport services, the behaviour of consumers (see Gilbert 1991) and the outcome in terms of use and profitability for producers. It is within this context that Buckley's (1987) research proves useful in understanding the nature of relationships which may exist in the supply chain.

From Buckley's four chains (Figure 5.1), it is evident that a variety of distribution systems exists for the sale and consumption of transport services. One of the critical issues in the distribution system for the seller is access to superior information on available services, so that these can be sold to the consumer. There are various studies which document tourism and transport retailing (e.g. Holloway and Plant 1988), where the agent or broker is normally paid a commission on their sales. The travel agent comprises a convenient one-stop location for tourists to buy tourism services as an inclusive package, which includes transport and accommodation, usually marketed through the medium of a brochure. The packaging of these products or services (much of the literature interchanges these terms) by wholesalers (e.g. tour operators) reduces the tourists' transaction costs of purchasing each element independently. Thus a travel agent normally receives around 10 per cent for a sale of a holiday marketed by a tour operator, but the overall cost to the consumer is markedly lower than arranging the same components independently. The tour operator is able to reduce the number of

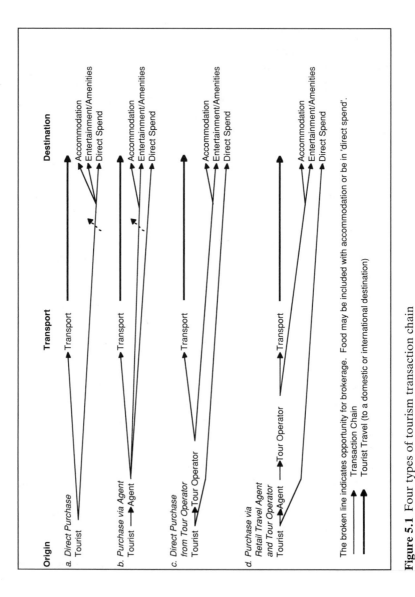

Figure 5.1 Four types of tourism transaction chain

Source: After Witt *et al.* (1991: 81).

transactions involved by packaging a holiday, thereby making economies in the supply through wholesale purchasing and by entering into long-term contracts with the suppliers of accommodation and transport services. Not only does this have benefits for the price charged to the purchaser, but it has more beneficial effects for the supplier as the number of intermediaries or brokers in the chain is eliminated by large tour operators and airlines who control a significant part of the distribution system. This has been the focus of innovative research by Bote Gómez and Sinclair (1991) who discuss the nature of corporations controlling the transaction chain to:

- maximise profit by eliminating costs
- reduce the price to the consumer to boost market share
- increase their level of concentration in the tourism industry.

Company strategies often pursue horizontal and vertical integration in the tourism and transport sectors, not only to control the production process of tourism services, but also to improve efficiency through economies of scale and long-term profitability. Although there are various economic theories to explain integration (see the excellent review by Bote Gómez and Sinclair 1991), the two terms – vertical and horizontal integration – have received little detailed analysis (Sinclair 1991).

Integration in the tourism sector: implications for the supply of tourist transport

According to Bote Gómez and Sinclair (1991):

- Integration is based on the concept of common ownership which may involve the co-ordination of, control of or no direct effect on the production process.
- Horizontal integration occurs where two enterprises with the same output merge to increase the companies' control over output. It can occur through mergers, acquisitions, collaboration, franchising agreements and more complex contractual arrangements and may induce concentration in the same business.
- Vertical integration occurs when an enterprise with different interests and involvement in the supply chain acquires or merges with companies contributing inputs to their activities, or where output purchasers provide a ready market for the service. This has the advantage of

decreasing economic uncertainty in the supply system and the avoidance of problems related to contract breaking.

The significance of integration in the UK tourism industry and the implications for tourist transport have been well documented by Sinclair (1991) and it is evident that:

> the transport function is an important point in the exchange of rights in the tourism transaction chain. If this function is subcontracted to an independent operator this delicate and central function can go out of control; hence the close integration of transport with other facilities in the integrated multinational company to ensure a degree of control in the distribution system in the supply of transport services to tourists.
>
> (Witt *et al.* 1991: 83)

Buckley (1987) notes that integration in tourist transport operations, especially vertical ownership, may help to reduce costs where higher load factors can be guaranteed for associated companies (e.g. Thomson Holidays in the UK can guarantee particular loads for its associated airline company – Britannia). Transaction analysis not only highlights the driving force in the supply system but also raises questions which researchers may wish to address in relation to specific companies and their role in tourist transport.

Furthermore, transaction analysis provides an opportunity to consider the changing patterns and processes shaping the tourist transport system and the growing internationalisation of the supply chain. The implications for service quality are notable because integration raises a fundamental problem for the tourist transport operator: if an independent airline becomes vertically integrated, should the parent company manage its operation even if it has no experience of this specialised activity? If not, how can the parent company ensure it controls both continuity and quality in the service encounter throughout the supply chain? This has been referred to as *total supply management*. In the area of corporate strategy, there is growing evidence that contractual arrangements are being used to ensure that service quality is a continuous process throughout the supply chain. For example, large companies such as Thomson Holidays are operated as independent organisations in the International Thomson group of companies which includes the sister company – Britannia Airlines – and its own travel agency chain – Lunn Poly. One option available to the group is to have a corporately administered system to ensure a particular benchmark in service quality for the tourist's experience is achieved throughout the supply chain. This would commence with the sale of a service via Lunn Poly, or direct through Thomson Holidays, and would include the flight and arrival in the destination, where a company representative meets tourists and travels with them on the airport transfer to their accommodation. This is then followed by a welcome where general information and a sales function is provided while promoting tours with coach companies endorsed by Thomson. During the holiday, the representative is empowered to deal with consumer issues in situ and to organise the return airport transfer for the departure. During the return flight, a corporate customer satisfaction questionnaire is administered by Thomson Holidays to assess the level of satisfaction with the package holiday, especially the transport element (see Figure 5.2). This provides a cheap form of market intelligence on corporate quality standards and may highlight areas for attention to reduce service interruptions and customer dissatisfaction.

Introducing a corporate quality control system may help to minimise customer dissatisfaction, particularly if the organisation employs and trains staff to deal with the service encounter as an ongoing process, rather than viewing the services as a series of discrete elements over which it has only a limited control. Yet even in a corporate quality control system, employees have to recognise the limit of their responsibilities and be able to refer customers to the relevant personnel empowered to deal with an interruption in the service requested. For example, this author recently experienced a service interruption on a charter flight to a Mediterranean destination with a large group of students on a study visit. A service which was requested was not provided because the chain of communication broke down between the tour operator, the handling agent at the airport and the airline. In this case the airline admitted the mistake but could not rectify the problem in-flight. Although it avoided a recurrence on the return flight, the fact that the interruption occurred provides a number of useful insights. For example, this author made a similar request for a particular service when travelling on another charter flight booked with the same tour operator. However, the difference was that the flight was on the company's own airline where the corporate quality control system was entirely handled by staff trained within the organisation. There were no service interruptions in this case and the airline's staff had a more consistent concern for service provision. This contrasted with the former

CUSTOMER SATISFACTION SURVEY

Dear Holidaymaker,

As a valued customer, your opinions of our holidays are extremely important in helping us to improve the standards and quality of future holidays.

If you are 17 years of age or over, we would be pleased if you would take a few minutes to complete this questionnaire.

Thank you for travelling with us and we look forward to seeing you again in the future.

Yours sincerely,

Thomson

▶ 1. YOUR HOLIDAY DETAILS *(For each question please tick appropriate box or where requested write in the answer.)*

A The name of your Resort or full name of Tour:

_____

B The name of your Accommodation i.e. the name of your Hotel/Villa/Apartment:

_____

C Board Arrangements

Full Board	1
Half Board	2
Bed/Breakfast	3
Self Catering	4
Room Only	5

(24)

D Holiday Length:

(number of nights)_____

E Departure from the UK:

Date _____ Month _____ 199 _____

F How long before the start of your holiday did you book?

Less than 4 weeks before	1
1-2 months before	2
3-4 months before	3
5-6 months before	4
7-8 months before	5
More than 9 months before	6

(94)

G Which of the following holidays was this one?

Thomson Summer Sun	1	Thomson Winter Sun	2	Wintersun Golfing	3
Horizon Selection	4	A La Carte	5	American Freedom	6
Discover Turkey	7	Faraway Shores	8	Florida Fun	9
Lakes & Mountains	10	Simply Greece	11	Ski Style	12
Ski Thomson	13	Small & Friendly	14	Sun Hotels	15
Tours	16	Villas & Apartments	17	Weddings in Paradise	18
Worldwide	19	Young at Heart	20	HCI	21
OSL	22	Skytours	23	Skytours Greece & Turkey	24
Square Deal	25	Price Breakers	26	Air Fares/ Flight Only	27
Other	99	*Please specify* _____ (109-110)		

H Are there any children aged 16 or under in your personal holiday party?

Yes ☐ 1   No ☐ 2   (103)

I Which smoking policy would you prefer on aircraft?

Smoking & non-smoking sections ☐ 1
Non-smoking only ☐ 2

(23)

Thomson   **HORIZON**   **Skytours**   OSL

Figure 5.2 Thomson Holidays customer satisfaction questionnaire

Copyright © Thomson Holidays, reproduced by permission.

carrier, where the cultural perceptions and virtual monopoly of flights to the destination meant that it did not need to adhere to the same quality standards.

In the case where the tour operator and purchaser of the transport service is unable directly to control the inputs and outputs throughout the system, one option may be to develop a contractually administered quality control system. Here all parties involved in the supply chain may make a contractual commitment to supply services to a certain standard to avoid weak links in the system (e.g. poor-quality food and service on-board an aircraft) which can affect the tourist's impression of the entire service. All parties involved need to agree on a particular quality principle (e.g. the British Standard 5750 for service systems which some transport operators, such as P & O European Ferries, already employ) to implement throughout the supply chain, using performance indicators to ensure the necessary standards are being reached. One way of examining the supply chain for specific tourist transport operators which are public companies is to examine their annual report. For this reason, it is pertinent to consider the role of such data sources, their purpose and how they may be used.

Analysing annual reports: company accounts

An annual report is used by companies to provide a review of the year's activities and it contains company accounts which are prepared within accounting guidelines in force in the country where the head office is based. For example, in the case of SIA, the accounts must be deposited in Singapore.

Bird and Rutherford (1989) argue that company accounts contain messages which use specialist jargon to deal with a complex situation. Once the specialist jargon is decoded by the reader, company accounts provide an insight into the financial performance of businesses. As Bird and Rutherford (1989) explain, there are the following key elements within company accounts:

- a balance sheet
- a profit and loss account

Within the balance sheet, items of value (assets) are listed and any claims against them are set out. A claim is a liability, such as an unpaid bill. Assets are divided into:

- fixed assets, which are those acquired for use within the business
- current assets, comprising cash and other items which are to be converted into cash.

Liabilities within the accounts are also divided into current, where their settlement will be made within 1 year, and long-term liabilities to be settled after 1 year.

It should be recognised that a balance sheet only provides a snapshot of an organisation's activities at one point in time. Therefore, analysts tend to consider company accounts over a 3 to 5 year period to give a more realistic assessment of an organisation's business performance.

There is a great deal of debate among accountants over the reliability of such documents, owing to the degree of creative accounting which exists within such documents. In other words, critics argue that company accounts only record what a company wants to state publicly about its activities. In fact one can argue that the flexibility and vagueness of accounting rules in relation to the preparation of company accounts and financial results mean that they are no longer an absolute measure of success. Manipulation of the profit and loss account and the balance sheet to report flattering results which meet corporate investors' and stock markets' expectations have contributed to the pressure for creative accounting. Notwithstanding these limitations associated with company accounts within published annual reports, they provide an important public relations function for companies and offer an insight into the organisation, operation and scale of a company's activities.

Case study 7: Singapore International Airlines and the supply of tourist transport services

> One interesting way to identify the extent to which integration exists within the tourist transport system is to consider one company and its activities. The case of Singapore International Airlines (SIA) provides a useful example since it is based within one of the fastest growing tourism markets in the 1990s – the Pacific Rim (Edwards 1992). SIA was also one of the most profitable international airlines in 1990/1 (Humphries 1992) and its transformation from a state-owned enterprise (SOE) to a privatised company has been the focus of recent research (Sikorski

Case study 7 (*continued*)

Table 5.1 Key features of the SIA Annual Report

- Chairman's Statement
- Corporate Data
- Statistical Highlights
- Operating Review
- Aviation Relations
- Subsidiaries
- Fleet and Route Network
- Financial Review
- Sensitivity Analysis
- Report by the Board of Directors
- Profit and Loss Accounts
- Balance Sheets
- Statements of Changes in Financial Position
- Notes to the Accounts
- Auditors' Report
- Five-Year Financial Summary of the Group
- Ten-Year Statistical Record of the Company
- Shareholding Statistics
- Share Price and Turnover
- Major Properties of the Group

Source: Modified from SIA (1992) Contents Page.

1990). As a tourist transport operator, SIA has been widely regarded as Singapore's premier enterprise, formed in 1947, developing as the national flag carrier in 1972 and privatised after 1985. It has consistently performed as a profitable enterprise and the close relationship with the government has meant it has developed a synergy with the Singapore Tourism Promotion Board to assist with the development of incoming tourism.

Sikorski (1990) provides a detailed analysis of how SIA was developed and financed as well as its route to privatisation. Since the development of SIA is dealt with elsewhere, this case study focuses on one data source – SIA's Annual Report for 1991/2 – to illustrate the scope and involvement of one company in the supply chain for transport and tourism services.

Table 5.2 SIA fleet and aircraft orders at 31 March 1992

Aircraft	Engine	In operation	On firm order	Reconfirmable	On option
B747-400 (MEGATOP)*	PW 4056	12	25	–	13
B747-300 (BIG TOP)	PW JT9D-7R4G2	11	–	–	–
B747-300 Combi	PW JT9D-7R4G2	3	–	–	–
B747-200 Freighter	PW JT9D-7R4G2	2	1	–	–
B747-400 Freighter	PW 4056	–	2	–	4
B747-200	PW JT9D-7Q	4	–	–	–
A310-300	PW 4152	10	5	–	0
A310-200	PW JT9D-7R4EI	6	–	–	–
A340-300	CFM 56-5C4	–	7	7	6
TOTAL		48	40	7	23

Notes: Average age of fleet: 5 years 1 month (as at 31 March 1992).

* 1st order in March 1986: 14 firm, 6 on option;
  2nd order in January 1990: 15 firm, 15 on option;
  3rd order in March 1991: 6 firm.
PW = Pratt and Whitney.
CFM = GEC/CFM.

Source: SIA (1992: 63).

Case study 7 (*continued*)

The SIA Annual Report

The SIA Annual Report for 1991/2 comprises 139 pages and some of the key themes are listed in Table 5.1. As a source of information on tourist transport, one has to wade through the public relations material to assess the statistical information provided. As an accessible data source for researchers, it is a baseline of information from which further research can be undertaken. The initial statistical highlights within the report provide an executive summary of the company accounts, but it is the discussion of the SIA group activities which is the most informative in terms of airline operations and integration within its business activities.

The 'Operating Review' discusses the company's performance as the activities of the SIA group saw its operating profit increase by 2.6 per cent to Singapore $976 million for 1991/2 as passenger traffic increased by 13.1 per cent. Some of the factors which underpinned the SIA group's performance were route development, consolidating its position in the Pacific, adding a fifth destination (Sendai) to its Japanese routes and further expansion in SE Asia, especially Malaysia. The re-establishment of a service to Vietnam, for the first time since the Vietnam War, and increased frequencies on other long-haul routes (e.g. the UK and Australia) led to the airline's continued international growth. To support route development, an airline's fleet needs to keep pace with the demands placed upon it. Table 5.2 illustrates the scale of SIA's major investment programme in fleet modernisations and expansion, particularly the large number of non-stop long-haul (e.g. Boeing 747-400s) and medium-haul aircraft (e.g. Airbus A310-300s) it aimed to acquire. The total cost of SIA's 56 747-400s was US $10 billion and orders for four additional A310s in May 1991 were valued at US $347 million. Furthermore, SIA's intention to acquire a further 20 Airbus A340-300s is also valued at US $3.355 billion, to be delivered between 1995 and 1998.

Case study 7 (*continued*)

Table 5.3 SIA subsidiary and associated companies at 31 March 1992

	Activities	*Country of incorporation and place of business*
SUBSIDIARY COMPANIES		
Singapore Airport Terminal Services (Private) Limited	Investment holding company	Singapore
SATS Apron Services Pte Ltd	Airport apron services	Singapore
SATS Airport Services Pte Ltd (previously known as SATS Cargo Services Pte Ltd)	Airport cargo services	Singapore
SATS Catering Pte Ltd	Catering services	Singapore
SATS Passenger Services Pte Ltd	Airport passenger services	Singapore
SATS Security Services Pte Ltd	Security services	Singapore
SilkAir (Singapore) Private Limited (previously known as Tradewinds Private Limited)	Air transportation	Singapore
Tradewinds Tours & Travel Private Limited	Tour wholesaling	Singapore
Singapore Aviation and General Insurance Company (Pte) Ltd	Aviation insurance	Singapore
SIA Engineering Company Private Limited (previously known as Singapore Engine Overhaul Centre Private Limited)	Engine overhaul and related services	Singapore
SIA Properties (Pte) Ltd	Provision of building services	Singapore
Singapore Airport Duty-Free Emporium (Private) Limited	Sale of duty-free goods	Singapore
Singapore Flying College Pte Ltd	Training of pilots	Singapore

Case study 7 (continued)

Table 5.3 *Continued*

	Activities	*Country of incorporation and place of business*
SUBSIDIARY COMPANIES		
Abacus Travel Systems Pte Ltd	Marketing of Abacus reservations systems	Singapore
Singapore Jamco Private Limited	Manufacture of aircraft cabin equipment	Singapore
Aero Laundry & Linen Services Private Limited	Laundry services	Singapore
Cargo Community Network Pte Ltd	Provision and marketing of cargo community systems	Singapore
Star Kingdom Investment Limited	Real estate	Hong Kong
SATS (Curaçao) N.V.	Catering services	Netherlands Antilles
SH Tours Ltd	Tour wholesaling	United Kingdom
Auspice Limited	Investment company	Channel Islands
ASSOCIATED COMPANIES		
Singapore Airport Bus Services Ltd	Taxi services	Singapore
Loyang Valley Pte Ltd	Property development	Singapore
Island Cruises (S) Pte Ltd	Dormant company	Singapore
Service quality (SQ) Centre Pte Ltd	Quality service training	Singapore
Maldives Inflight Catering Private Limited	Catering services	Maldives

Source: SIA (1992: 103).

Case study 7 (*continued*)

Integration in SIA group activities

The global scale and distribution of airline services has now become increasingly dependent upon computer reservation systems (CRSs) for marketing (Holloway 1989). These CRSs have been developed by airlines and account for the majority of airline bookings in North America and Europe. SIA has participated in this recent expansion in CRSs (Archdale 1991) to expand its products to retail travel agents whilst encouraging other airlines to join its system to market their services. By January 1992, the following partners had joined SIA's 'Abacus' CRS:

- SIA
- Cathay Pacific
- China Airlines
- Malaysia Airlines
- Philippine Airlines
- Royal Brunei Airlines
- SilkAir (an SIA subsidiary)
- All Nippon Airways
- WorldSpan (a CRS owned by Delta, Northwest and Transworld Airlines)

According to SIA, Abacus is the major CRS in Brunei, Hong Kong, Malaysia, the Philippines, Singapore and Taiwan and is being extended to Korea and Australia to improve the distribution of airline services on a global basis.

The subsidiary and associated companies of the SIA group and their main activities are shown in Table 5.3 which highlights the involvement in the tourist transport system, particularly:

- tour wholesaling (package holidays)
- aviation insurance
- air transport (SilkAir)
- airport services (catering, airport ownership, security services)
- duty-free sales
- airport bus services
- CRS (Abacus Travel Systems)

Case study 7 (*continued*)

Table 5.4 SIA company expenditure 1991/2

	1991/2		1990/1		Change
	$M	%	$M	%	%
Staff costs	1,036	25.0	831	22.1	+ 24.5
Fuel and oil costs	704	17.0	780	20.8	− 9.8
Depreciation charges	614	14.8	513	13.6	+ 19.8
Handling charges	365	8.8	316	8.4	+ 15.6
Aircraft maintenance and overhaul costs	279	6.7	263	7.0	+ 6.4
In-flight meal costs	235	5.7	220	5.9	+ 6.5
Landing and parking fees	231	5.5	204	5.4	+ 13.3
Others	685	16.5	633	16.8	+ 8.2
	4,149	100.0	3,760	100.0	+ 10.3

Source: SIA (1992: 72).

- aircraft engineering and maintenance
- hotel ownership (SIA Properties)
- quality service training

SIA's subsidiary companies' activities are reported separately in the annual report although the majority of the document focuses on SIA. For example, the Financial Review of SIA identifies revenue generated, expenditure (Table 5.4), the capacity and break-even load factor (the point at which an aircraft makes a profit), as well as detailed accounting information for the group (e.g. taxation, dividends, the financial position, balance sheet, liabilities and assets). From an aviation perspective, the route performance of the airline in Asia, Europe, the Americas and the south west Pacific provides a useful summary of how specific markets are performing (see Table 5.5). SIA also undertakes a 'Sensitivity Analysis' which focuses on key indicators: revenue, staff costs, fuel and oil costs, company staff productivity and SIA group staff strength and productivity with a breakdown by the geographical areas in which the airline operates.

Case study 7 (*continued*)

Table 5.5 SIA airline operations by routes

	Revenue ($M)		Overall load factor (%)		Passenger seat factor (%)	
	1991–2	*1990–1*	*1991–2*	*1990–1*	*1991–2*	*1990–1*
Asia	1,931	1,567	64.9	66.7	73.3	73.4
Europe	1,305	1,421	72.2	73.6	73.1	76.9
Americas	1,032	922	71.0	72.1	74.8	77.0
SW Pacific	574	578	72.5	69.7	72.3	71.0
Systemwide	4,842	4,488	69.9	71.0	73.5	75.1

Non-scheduled services and incidental revenue

	171	114
	5,013	4,602

Route performance in Asia

Asia was the largest contributor to revenue, with a growth of $364 million or 23.2% to $1,931 million. Traffic rose 24.7% against a 28.1% increase in capacity from additional frequencies, new services introduced, and the resumption of flights suspended during the Gulf crisis. Overall load factor dropped 1.8 points to 64.9%. Frequency increases were mounted to Colombo, Madras, Karachi, Bombay, Mali, Mauritius, Kuala Lumpur, Penang, Denpasar, Fukuoka, Hong Kong, Taipei, Seoul and Beijing/Shanghai. New services were launched to Sendai, Surabaya, Ho Chi Minh City and Johannesburg. Yield fell 1.2% as a result of the strong Singapore dollar.

Source: SIA (1992: 87–8).

It is evident that company annual reports can be a useful data source from which to examine not only integration in the tourist transport system but also the performance of individual companies. Annual reports are an accessible data source which can be obtained direct from public companies' head offices. Although the amount of detailed information contained within annual reports may be somewhat daunting and complex, analysis of such sources will yield important insights into the commercial, operational and supply aspects of different tourist transport operators.

Having outlined the scope of one company's involvement in the supply chain within the tourist transport system, attention now turns to how the state may radically alter the supply system through the relaxation of regulatory measures.

The state and the supply of tourist transport: airline deregulation in the USA

Air travel is a major form of tourist transport since 30 per cent of international travellers use air as the main form of transport (Mann and Mantel 1992). International air travel provides an interesting example of how government policy (see Chapter 3) has led to different effects upon the supply of transport services for tourists. Sealy (1992) identifies two approaches ranging from:

- a regulated transport system where a country exercises sovereignty over its airspace
- a liberalised and unregulated system characterised by an open-skies policy.

In Chapter 3, it was clear that various historical and political factors may explain the aviation policy in a given country. The regulations governing airline operations by international bodies such as ICAO and IATA (see Holloway 1989; Mill 1992) and bilateral agreements were influential in shaping air travel in a regulated environment until the late 1970s (see Table 5.6). In addition to IATA (the United Nations body which facilitates the international regulation of air travel), national level governments play an active role in regulating air travel.

The experiences in the USA with domestic airline deregulation in 1978 led to a complete re-evaluation of the supply of air travel in terms of its organisation, operation and regulation by the state. The lessons of deregulation in North America were also a testbed for aviation strategies subsequently developed in Australia and those planned for the EC. The case of the US domestic airline market is also interesting because 'it is more highly developed and more extensively used in the United States than in any other part of the world' (Graham 1992: 188). For example, in 1988 air travel in the USA exceeded 1.7 billion passenger kilometres and is set to increase to 2.2 billion by the year 2000. According to Button (1991), the implications for the supply of tourist transport can be examined in relation to:

Table 5.6 International co-operation in air travel

International air travel requires countries to co-operate so that the movement of aircraft and people can occur in a reasonably flexible manner. To provide a degree of regulation and coherence to air travel, two important international agreements underpin present-day air travel:

- The 1944 Chicago Convention, which established the principle of freedoms of the air.
- The 1946 Bermuda Agreement, which provided a framework for bilateral agreements to implement freedoms of the air. A bilateral agreement is where two countries agree to provide an air service on a reciprocal basis and it helps to facilitate and protect the rights of each country's airline irrespective of whether it is a profit or non-profit venture.

Consequently, the following 'Freedoms of the Air' can be observed:

Freedom 1: the right of an airline to fly over one country to get to another.
Freedom 2: the right of an airline to stop in another country for fuel/maintenance but not to pick up or drop off passengers.
Freedom 3: the right of an airline to drop off in a foreign country traffic from the country in which it is registered, to a separate country.
Freedom 4: the right of an airline to carry back passengers from a foreign country to the country in which it is registered.
Freedom 5: the right of an airline to carry back passengers between two foreign countries as long as the flight originates or terminates in the country in which it is registered.
Freedom 6: the right of an airline to carry passengers to a gateway in the country in which it is registered and then on to a foreign country, where neither the origin nor the ultimate destination is the country in which it is registered.
Freedom 7: the right of an airline to operate entirely outside of the country in which it is registered in carrying passengers between two other countries.
Freedom 8: the right of an airline, registered in a foreign country, to carry passengers between two points in the same foreign country.

Note: According to Mill (1992) the first *two* freedoms are accepted internationally while freedoms 3–6 are the subject of bilateral agreements and the last two freedoms are rarely accepted.

Source: Based on Mill (1992: 81).

- the corporate response of airline companies to the new competitive environment for air travel
- the effect on the functioning of the transport system
- the effect on consumers, service provision and service quality
- the impact upon complementary infrastructure (e.g. airports).

To understand the impact of deregulation of the domestic market for air travel in the USA, it is pertinent to examine the regulatory framework prior to and following deregulation as a context in which to consider the changes on the supply of air services.

Airline regulation in the USA

In the USA, airline regulation can be dated to the 1930s and the passage of the 1938 Civil Aeronautics Act and the subsequent formation of the Civil Aeronautics Board (CAB) in 1946 which licensed routes and airline operations, regulated the pricing of fares and monitored safety issues. The federal regulation of civil aviation was firmly established within a government department. It also limited the number of domestic carriers until the 1970s to avoid overcompetition. Despite such measures, the post-war boom in domestic and international air travel in the USA was facilitated by a buoyant economy, innovation in aircraft design, reduced travel costs and stable fares maintained by the CAB. In addition, the CAB provided subsidies for local service carriers so that small communities could be connected to the emerging inter-urban trunk network of air routes, to achieve social equity in access to air travel. This also facilitated the development of major airlines as the CAB guaranteed loans for carriers who invested in new aircraft to serve such routes. To reduce subsidy payments, carriers were gradually awarded more lucrative longer-haul routes with a view to carriers cross-subsidising the shorter feeder routes from small communities to connect with trunk routes. These developments occurred against the background of pressure from the airline industry to increase fares in the 1970s, which appeared to place the consumer at a disadvantage. In 1975, the CAB began to relax some of its restrictions on the operation and pricing of charter aircraft to compete with scheduled flights, permitted discounted fares and licensed new transatlantic carriers prepared to offer low fares. This provided the background for the 1978 Airline Deregulation Act which established greater flexibility in route licensing and abolished the CAB in 1984. As a result, some of the CAB's functions were transferred to the Department of Transportation, including responsibility for:

- the negotiation of international air transport rights and licensing of US carriers to serve the airline market
- the monitoring of international fares
- the maintenance of air services to small communities
- consumer affairs and complaints
- airline mergers.

In contrast, the Federal Aviation Administration (FAA) powers included:

- the promotion of air safety and use of navigable airspace
- regulations on the competence of pilots and airworthiness of aircraft
- the operation of air traffic control systems.

From these regulatory responsibilities it is evident that the structure of the US airline business comprises:

- airlines
- airports and providers of air traffic control facilities
- aircraft manufacturers (e.g. Boeing and McDonnell Douglas)
- consumers
- third parties, such as government agencies (e.g. FAA and Department of Transportation).

In the case of the airline business in the USA, Shaw (1982: 74) identifies the following structure for airline companies:

- the majors – earning in excess of $1 billion per annum
- the nationals – based on a regional network
- new entrants
- small regional and commuter airlines which provide the short-haul link-ups with the majors to feed into their networks.

How has deregulation affected the supply of air transport?

The effects of deregulation on the supply of tourist transport

Within the literature on the supply of tourist transport, one area which has been well researched is airline deregulation. This has focused on the controversy over the effect of such measures on the commercial environment for airline operations and there is not space within this chapter to review the specialised range of papers generated by researchers on this issue. One approach is to consider a limited number of issues which are constantly referred to by researchers. According to the US Department of Transportation, following deregulation the number of carriers serving the USA increased from 36 in 1978 to 72 in 1980 and 86 in 1985, dropping to 60 by 1990 (including air cargo carriers) (see Table 5.7). However, a range of factors such as financial insolvency, mergers and acquisitions reduced the number of operators to ten carriers of regional or national scale by 1988. This was followed by a period of consolidation, and by 1991 the situation had worsened with both Pan Am and Eastern Airlines having faced bankruptcy: the existing carriers had either prospered or lost market share to competitors (see Table 5.7). Thus a 62 per cent increase in the number of domestic travellers carried on US airlines during 1978–90 has been followed by a greater degree of concentration and integration in the airline business. What has this meant for the structure and provision of services through US airline networks?

From the transport geographer's perspective, a distinctive spatial structure in air travel has emerged in the USA (see Chou 1993 and Shaw 1993) whereby the major US airlines have developed a hub and spoke structure as spatial and commercial strategies for organising airline operations in a deregulated environment. This contrasts with the CAB regulation era where inter-urban routes were often 805 km or more in length and little attention was given to integrating the route networks among operators. However, in a deregulated environment where cost reductions became a central element of the commercial strategy, least-cost solutions and network maximisation are a priority to achieve efficient operations. Airline services need to be responsive to demand and there has been a greater emphasis on airlines connecting all the nodes in their network. In this context, a 'hub' and 'spoke' system of provision (Figure 5.3) may enable airlines to serve a large number of people over a wide area, the hub acting as a switching point for passengers travelling on feeder routes along the spokes which cannot support a trunk route.

According to O'Kelly (1986) hubs are least-cost solutions for airlines and may combine a range of airports in a region, assisting the airline in running a high-frequency service along trunk routes between hubs. Along the spokes, regional carriers, often code sharing under the 'majors' identification, provide the feeder services. The result has been a geographical concentration of airline hubs in major US cities, based on historical ties with certain airports, airline mergers, the servicing of niche tourist markets and responses to competitors, so that major operators provide between 100 and 200 departures each day from some of the key hubs. Thus, a spatial concentration among the six largest airlines has occurred, leading to the development of four major hub cities – Atlanta, Chicago, Dallas and Denver (see Figure 5.4). This was illustrated in Shaw's (1993) recent analysis where the following national hubs emerged (with the regional hubs in brackets):

• *American Airlines* – Dallas/Fort Worth and Chicago (Nashville and Raleigh/Durham)

Table 5.7 Airlines providing inter-state jet service during the deregulation era

Origin and name	Began service *	Date	Status
Trunk carriers (11)			
American	pre-1978	1989	1st ranking carrier**
Braniff	pre-1978	1982	Ceased operation due to bankruptcy
		1984	Resumed limited service
		1989	Ceased operation due to bankruptcy
Continental	pre-1978	1989	6th ranking carrier (under Texas Air Corp)
Delta	pre-1978	1989	2nd ranking carrier
Eastern	pre-1978	1989	Declared bankruptcy; conducting limited operations (under Texas Air Corp)
National	pre-1978	1980	Acquired by PanAm
NorthWest	pre-1978	1989	5th ranking carrier
PanAm	pre-1978	1989	12th ranking carrier
TWA	pre-1978	1989	8th ranking carrier
United	pre-1978	1989	3rd ranking carrier
Western	pre-1978	1986	Acquired by Delta
Local service carriers (8)			
Frontier	pre-1978	1985	Acquired by People Express
Hughes Airwest	pre-1978	1980	Acquired by Republic
North Central	pre-1978	1979	Merged within Southern to form Republic
		1986	Republic acquired by NorthWest
Ozark	pre-1978	1986	Acquired by TWA
Piedmont	pre-1978	1987	Acquired by USAir
Southern	pre-1978	1979	Merged with North Central to form Republic
		1986	Republic acquired by NorthWest
Texas International	pre-1978	1982	Acquired by Continental
USAir	pre-1978	1989	4th ranking carrier
Intra-state carriers (5)			
Alaska	pre-1978	1989	15th ranking carrier
AirCal	1979	1987	Acquired by American
Air Florida	1979	1984	Ceased operation due to bankruptcy
		1985	Acquired by Midway
PSA	1979	1987	Acquired by USAir
Southwest	1979	1989	9th ranking carrier
Charter carriers (2)			
Capitol	1979	1984	Ceased operation due to bankruptcy
World	1979	1985	Ceased operation due to bankruptcy

Table 5.7 *Continued*

Origin and name	Began service *	Date	Status
Commuter carriers (3)			
Air Wisconsin	1982	1989	18th ranking carrier
Empire	1980	1986	Acquired by Piedmont
Horizon	1983	1986	Acquired by Alaska
New carriers (17)			
Air Atlanta	1984	1986	Ceased operation due to bankruptcy
Air One	1983	1984	Ceased operation due to bankruptcy
American International	1982	1984	Ceased operation due to bankruptcy
America West	1983	1989	11th ranking carrier
Florida Express	1984	1988	Acquired by Braniff
Frontier Horizon	1984	1985	Ceased operation due to bankruptcy
Hawaii Express	1982	1983	Ceased operation due to bankruptcy
Jet America	1982	1986	Acquired by Alaska
Midway	1979	1989	16th ranking carrier
Muse (Transtar)	1981	1985	Acquired by Southwest
New York Air	1980	1985	Acquired by Continental
Northeastern	1982	1984	Ceased operation due to bankruptcy
Pacific East	1982	1984	Ceased operation due to bankruptcy
Pacific Express	1982	1984	Ceased operation due to bankruptcy
People Express	1981	1986	Acquired by Continental
Presidential	1985	1987	Became feeder carrier for United
Sunworld	1983	1988	Ceased operation due to bankruptcy

Notes: * Date carrier began inter-state service with jet aircraft.
    ** Size ranking based on passengers carried during 12 months ended September 1989.
Source: Button (1991). Copyright © David Fulton Publishers.

- *Delta* – Atlanta, Cincinnati, Dallas/Fort Worth (Salt Lake City)
- *USAir* – Pittsburgh and Charlotte (Baltimore and Philadelphia)
- *United Airlines* – Chicago (Washington, DC and Denver)
- *NorthWest Airlines* – Detroit, Memphis, Minneapolis/St Paul
- *Continental Airlines* – Houston, New York, Denver and Cleveland

Figure 5.4 also incorporates two other hubs (Los Angeles and San Francisco) of lesser significance in the overall pattern of airline routes to illustrate the principal airports serving the western seaboard.

In spatial terms, Continental Airlines' network covers a wide area within the USA, while Delta's network is heavily concentrated in the southern states with regional hubs serving the western seaboard. In contrast, NorthWest Airlines serves the Mid West, while United

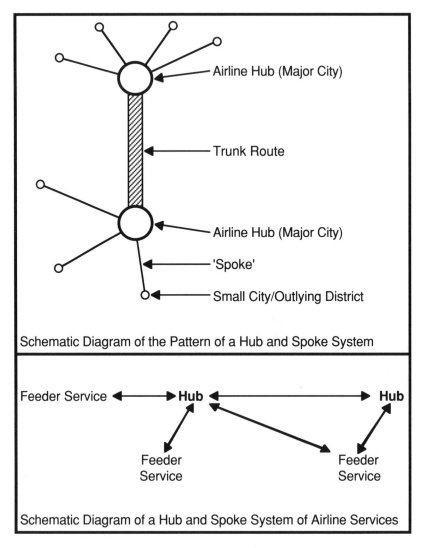

Schematic Diagram of the Pattern of a Hub and Spoke System

Schematic Diagram of a Hub and Spoke System of Airline Services

Figure 5.3 Schematic distribution of a hub and spoke system

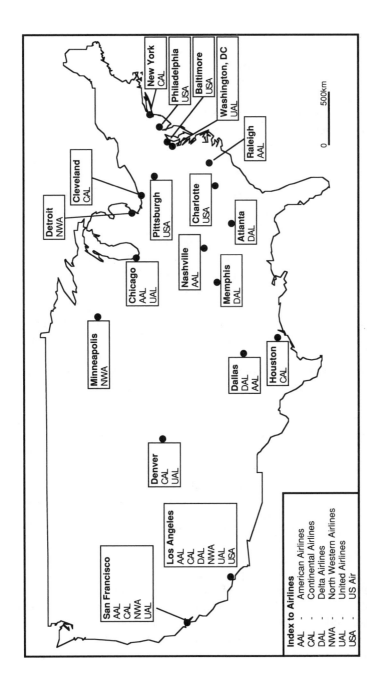

Figure 5.4 Distribution of major airline hubs in the USA

Source: After Shaw (1993).

Airlines has hubs located on an east–west axis across the USA, offering the best connections to cities in the western seaboard. USAir, however, has four hubs in close proximity, owing to its interest in the east-coast market. Shaw (1993) observes that USAir is unique as it operates many other nodes as smaller hubs to serve other areas. This is one factor which has made the airline attractive to foreign airlines such as British Airways which took a $200 million stake in the airline in April 1993, providing it with a foothold in the lucrative North American and trans-atlantic market.

Following deregulation, there has been a considerable debate among researchers over the effect on consumers (tourists and non-tourists). For example, Kihl (1988) argues that deregulation led to a decline in service quality as smaller communities not directly connected to trunk routes faced fare increases and less frequent services. It is clear that airline mergers may have led to a decline in the number of carriers serving some communities, but Jemiolo and Oster (1981) maintained that any changes in service provision to less accessible communities were a result of recession and greater fuel costs rather than deregulation. Similar debates also concern the effect of deregulation on passenger safety (Moses and Savage 1990). Golich (1988) asserts that the development of hubbing operations led to a decline in safety as more services and take-offs/landings were concentrated into specific areas, increasing the potential for accidents. However, the US civil aviation statistics for the period 1975–90 show that the number of fatalities actually dropped from 663 to 424, while the rate per million aircraft miles flown has remained constant at 0.001 for scheduled services. However, Golich's (1988) assessment may have a great deal of validity in view of the congested nature of many US airports which is discussed later.

Following deregulation and the growth in new entrants to the domestic airline market, consumer complaints increased to a peak of 40,985 in 1987 but dropped to 6,126 for 1991. The most commonly reported problems in 1991 which caused dissatisfaction were:

- flight problems, such as cancellations and delays (30.7 per cent)
- baggage problems (14.5 per cent)
- problems associated with refunds (12.8 per cent)
- customer service issues such as unhelpful employees, inadequate meals and poor cabin service (11.7 per cent)
- errors in ticketing and reservations (10.8 per cent)
- incorrect or incomplete information about fares (6.3 per cent)

- the process of 'bumping' passengers off overbooked flights (by offer-ing incentives not to travel on a specific flight) (5 per cent)
- other reasons (passengers smoking and advertising) (8.2 per cent)

(from US Department of Transportation, Office of Consumer Fares, cited in *US Statistical Yearbook* 1992).

Transport analysts, however, have pointed to the growing degree of concentration in the airline business in the USA following deregulation (Table 5.7). The consequences for consumer choice are that for certain cities there is little choice of airline, which has assisted the larger carriers to improve their income, though not necessarily their profitability (Morrison and Winston 1986). Airlines have exercised greater control over their workforce in pursuit of continued increases in productivity and greater economies of scale (Humphries 1992). Critics have also argued that deregulation has led to the larger carriers developing sophis-ticated marketing campaigns to foster customer loyalty to influence the choice of carrier through 'frequent flyer programmes' (Laws 1991) and the use of airline-controlled CRSs (Archdale 1991) to promote their services via travel retailers. Investment in technology and marketing tools to shape the pattern of supply to potential customers has also been reinforced through the hub and spoking operations of the 'majors'. For new entrants to gain a foothold in the US domestic airline market, not only would they need to secure a slot at an airport but they would need to be able to offer services to compete with the existing frequencies and service available. This would require major capital investment and commercial nerve at a time of considerable flux in the aviation market. Furthermore, Graham (1992) identifies the influence which major carriers exercise on hub airports, particularly their ability to limit new competition. Ironically, this has meant that hub airports have become less financially secure in the USA as restrictive practices such as 'majority-in-interest' (Graham 1992) may limit airport revenue gener-ation through the airlines' power of veto on capacity improvements to encourage competition.

The changes induced by deregulation have also had a pronounced effect on the US airport system as the demand for air travel has continued to grow despite constraints on the supply of airport capacity (Sealy 1992). Deregulation and the development of trunk routes and hubs have intensified congestion at major US airports. Sealy (1992) notes that 16 of the world's 25 leading airports handling in excess of 15 million passengers a year were in the USA. In 1992, eight US airports were constrained by lack of capacity which is expected to increase by a further nine airports in 1995 (see Doganis 1992: 15–24 for a fuller discussion of US airport output).

Having examined the effect of deregulation on the supply of air transport, attention now turns to the interface of supply and demand issues in relation to land-based tourist transportation systems in the Caribbean. For this reason, the example of Bermuda has been chosen to reflect some of the problems and management issues associated with tourist transport in a small island where the available space for tourism and transport competes and conflicts with other land uses.

The supply of tourist transport in destination areas

The supply of tourist transport services in the destination area is one area neglected in Buckley's (1987) transaction analysis. Two of the only studies which deal with this issue are Teye's (1992) study of Bermuda and Heraty's (1989) examination of supply-related problems which characterise less developed countries (LDCs). For this reason, the case of Bermuda is now considered, followed by an overview of the supply-related issues raised by Heraty (1989).

Land-based tourist transport systems: Bermuda

Tourism research on the Caribbean has generated a great deal of literature in learned journals such as *Tourism Management, Annals of Tourism Research* and more recently in publications by Gayle and Goodrich (1993) and Todd and Mather (1993). Whilst not wishing to reiterate the detailed research reported in these publications, the Caribbean is noteworthy as a major destination for over 10 million visitors from developed countries each year and is the focus of the world's cruise ship business (Lawton and Butler 1987; Peisley 1992a; Dickinson 1993). Therefore, it is an appropriate area to focus upon, particularly as tourist arrivals increased by 40.3 per cent in 1985–90 while world tourist arrivals only increased by 25 per cent, generating $96 billion in gross expenditure for the region in 1990 (Gayle and Goodrich 1993).

Research by Archer (1989) considers the economic impact and volume of tourism in the Caribbean basin and how international arrivals and cruise ship arrivals affected the economy of small islands. The literature on small-island tourism is still developing (Pearce 1987), but Wilkinson's (1989) analysis of such small-island microstates provides a useful review into:

- ways of classifying small islands
- why tourism has assumed such a prominent role
- the problems related to scale and size on small islands
- the impact of external influences seeking to control the supply chain (e.g. multinational corporations and overseas investment companies).

The effect of multinational corporations on microstates was reviewed by Britton (1982) in relation to tour operators, airlines and hotel corporations which seize development and marketing opportunities to control the tourism economy through foreign ownership. Bermuda is an interesting example in this context. Wilkinson (1989) notes that its relatively strong economic and political will to restrict the large-scale expansion of tourism led to a moratorium on new hotels and limits on the number of cruise ships entering the harbour at any one time.

The development of tourism in microstates such as Bermuda has generated a requirement for a land-based tourist transport system to facilitate development and the movement of visitors around the island. Although infrastructure provision is not without environmental impacts (Holder 1988), Bermuda is a good example where research into the role of tourist transport has led to a better understanding of the interface of transport and tourism and the conflicts they can cause.

Case study 8: The tourist transport system in Bermuda

Bermuda comprises almost 150 small islands in the Caribbean, although only 20 are actually inhabited. A series of bridges and causeways connect the main islands where approximately 62,000 people live in an area of 55 km². It is unique within the Caribbean due to its high per capita income of $22,540 (1987) which is greater than both the USA and Switzerland (Teye 1992). Such prosperity derives from:

- international businesses in the islands
- military bases
- tourism, which is the largest contributor to the economy.

Case study 8 (*continued*)

The high-spending markets (e.g. the North Americans) attracted to the islands require good-quality transport links (air and sea) and a transport network which is co-ordinated and efficient. The reliance upon land transportation for tourists within the destination to provide airport/port transfers to resorts, transport to tourist attractions and sightseeing has a major impact on the transport system on the islands.

One of the main concerns which Teye (1992) observes was the decline of the islands' railway system and the growth in car ownership which stimulated the development of the country's road network. As in many microstates, cars have become the symbol of economic prosperity, yet space constraints and the continued development of roads have contributed to high densities of car ownership (e.g. 220 vehicles per kilometre in Bermuda) with associated environmental impacts. Bermuda's government examined the problem posed by private car ownership in the 1970s and 1980s and the complex nature of transport planning for residents and tourism (see Teye 1992: 399–400 for a detailed analysis of government research on the issue). The principal measures within Bermuda's transport policy have been to regulate ownership through licensing, speed controls and limits on vehicle replacement. The consequences for tourist transport are restrictions on car hire which have led to an expansion in motorcycle and moped use. This has led to significant conflicts between the use of mopeds (less than 50cc engine size) by tourists for sightseeing and touring, and local traffic. For example, in 1970 there were 3,296 accidents and 24 fatalities, although a crash helmet law in 1977 and improved traffic education for tourists by moped hire companies led to a significant reduction in the number of accidents.

In common with many other small islands which have developed tourism, Bermuda has traffic problems related to non-tourist (commuting) and tourist travel to the capital city (Hamilton) and tourist travel within tourist zones and corridors along the south shore where much of the tourist accommodation is located (Figure 5.5). Given the primary role of Hamilton as a commercial and entertainment centre and the hub of the island's bus services,

Case study 8 (*continued*)

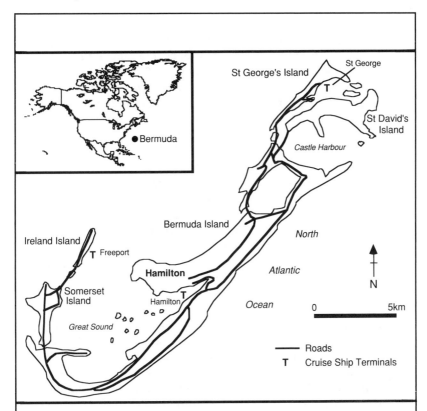

Figure 5.5 Bermuda: location and transport infrastructure

congestion generated by resident and tourist transport use is
virtually inevitable, without a decentralisation of these activities to
other areas.

Teye (1992) also notes the effect of seasonality in tourist movements on the islands (May–October) and the effect of cruise ships.
The cruise ship business in the Caribbean in the 1980s is well
documented by Lawton and Butler (1987) and within the context
of small islands there is widespread agreement that the arrival of
such ships can saturate small islands when the visitors disembark.

Case study 8 (*continued*)

Unlike other cruise ship ports, Bermuda has attracted long-stay visits (up to 4 days) where the ships dock and remain rather than arriving in the morning and leaving that evening. As a result, Teye (1992) argues that 'cruise ships in Bermuda literally become docked resorts'. Yet prior to 1984, up to seven cruise ships a week were docking in Bermuda. The impact on the tourist transport system results in traffic congestion due to visitors renting taxis and for sightseeing.

One solution to manage this problem was the introduction in 1988 of limitations on cruise ship passengers by restricting the number of ships to four in port at any one time, and to restrict cruise ship visitors to 120,000, compared with 158,000 in 1987. This deliberate policy by Bermuda's government eliminated weekend cruise ships from docking, thereby reducing overcrowding and temporary congestion on the island's transport network. Therefore, this serves as a useful example of how the management of the supply of tourist transport infrastructure can induce a reduction in the demand.

One additional measure to manage tourist travel patterns in Bermuda which was adopted in government policy in 1973 was the development of tourist-specific routes (see Lew 1991 for a discussion of this concept). Although little progress has been made in this direction, Teye (1992) argues that the severity of the traffic problems facing the islands may require a clear strategy to designate a road hierarchy to reduce the conflict between the tourist and non-tourist use of roads. This would need to encourage the rational and managed touring of the islands' natural and man-made attractions and is preferable to further road building in a country already short of space. It is ironic that while tourism has generated prosperity for Bermudians, the symbol of success – the private car – is now posing major transport problems for the country in common with many other microstates which have followed tourism as a route to economic development. As Teye (1992: 405) readily acknowledges, 'most microstates have very few options if they allow poor transportation planning to destroy their tourist industry'.

Visitors expect good destination-specific transport systems and they form an important part of the tourist's overall experience of travel. For this reason, it is pertinent to focus on the issues raised by Heraty (1989) in the context of the LDCs in terms of how the supply of tourist transport needs to meet both the expectations and needs of visitors if the service encounter in the destination is to meet minimum standards. Although some of the problems Heraty (1989) examined are unique to LDCs, the general issues raised also have implications for developed countries. The issues which highlight tourists' expectations in the developed world and the maintenance of service quality, include:

Airport transfers   Tourists arriving in a destination after a tiring flight require convenient and comfortable transfer vehicles. The tendency to use a limited number of transfer vehicles to shuttle a large number of different tour groups to a dispersed range of hotels often adds to the inconvenience associated with long-haul travel in LDCs. The trend towards the use of baggage trucks to transport tourists' baggage to hotels owing to the lack of space on old vehicles is disconcerting for tourists and can cause delays due to misdelivery.

Sightseeing tours   For LDCs receiving high-spending tourists, one lucrative tourist transport service which offers potentially high profits to private operators is sightseeing tours. However, visitors from developed countries have high expectations for coaches with air conditioning, a public address system, which are safe and give good all-round visibility. In many cases, the capital cost of such vehicles is prohibitively expensive for private operators in LDCs who are forced to import such vehicles. Yet where they are provided, they significantly enhance the tourists' experience. The provision of well-trained tour guides, able to provide commentaries and answer questions in a variety of languages, is also an important asset. Guides who are able to convey the local culture, history, customs and lifestyle to visitors will be able to contribute to the tourists' memorable elements of their holiday, particularly if they provide adequate stopping places at cafes, restaurants or clearings with toilets and refreshment facilities.

Independent travel by tourists   The more adventurous tourist often wishes to travel on local public transport systems and adequate information needs to be made available (e.g. timetables). The use of hire cars is also a major tourist service in LDCs which need to be supplied according to a code of good practice. According to Heraty (1989: 289), good practice should include:

- high-quality vehicle standards, insurance and contract conditions
- provision of tourist-oriented maps and leaflets
- signposting of routes to tourist attractions and sights
- training for the police in dealing with tourist drivers
- action to address road-based and car-related crime affecting tourist hire cars
- safety standards for mopeds where governments permit tourists to hire such transport
- incentives to encourage short-stay visitors (e.g. cruise ship passengers) to venture away from the port to visit other locations
- licensing and regulation of taxi companies and drivers to prevent tourists being exploited.

From the transport policy-makers' perspective, Heraty (1989: 290) notes that in accommodating tourist transport needs, a range of problems need to be addressed at government level to facilitate tourist travel in destination areas, including:

- import duties, which may need to be relaxed to facilitate the acquisition of new vehicles and to make them more affordable and able to absorb 'standing costs' (when the vehicle is off the road) as tourist use declines outside of the peak season
- roads and tourist transport infrastructure need to be maintained to reduce wear and tear on vehicles
- skilled mechanics and vehicle drivers need to be trained to ensure an adequate supply of labour to meet demands
- traffic congestion related to peaked seasonal demand by tourists needs to be managed
- sufficient transport operators need to be licensed to prevent limited competition and cartel-type operations resulting under prohibitively expensive situations.

Summary

The supply of tourist transport services has attracted less attention than the analysis of demand issues. The use of transaction analysis provides a useful way to examine the supply chain in tourist transport systems and the contractual relationships which exist between consumers and suppliers. Such a framework provides a more analytical approach than the more empirical discussion which characterises many popular tourism textbooks. The discussion highlights the dominant influence of the tour operator sector in the supply of package holidays and the purchase of transport services on behalf of customers at discounted prices. The ability of tour wholesalers to negotiate discounts with transport operators reflects the capital-intensive nature of the tourist transport business and the need to achieve high load factors to improve profitability. This reflects the indivisible nature of transport operations discussed in Chapter 2, where airline companies cannot operate half of an aircraft if it is only 50 per cent full. The fixed costs of transport operations (e.g. repayments on loans to purchase capital equipment) mean that the incremental costs of selling existing capacity on a transport service are low once it has reached its break-even point. This is one explanation of the reduced price of airline tickets and standby fares as it is more efficient to sell a reduced-price ticket if the carrier has capacity than to underutilise the capacity. The contractual relationships associated with the supply of tourist transport are often negotiated up to 6 months in advance and a great deal of market planning goes into the provision of a service.

The provision of services which meet certain quality standards underlines one of the reasons why labour costs are so high in the supply of tourist transport services. It is a labour-intensive activity which requires staff contact with travellers to ensure their needs are met at each stage of travel. Employees cannot easily be substituted where a service is dependent on face to face contact with customers. Employee training and corporate human resource management policies (Baum 1993) are assuming an important role in ensuring that the supply of tourist transport services is based on a sound understanding of service quality, maximising customer satisfaction and developing programmes with incentives to foster customer loyalty. Analysis of company reports provides a useful source to assess both the role of the transport operator's involvement in the supply chain and their development of more sophisticated ways of serving the customer's needs.

The lessons of deregulation in the USA offer an insight into the way in which transport operators behave in a business environment free of state regulation, where profit is the ulterior motive for service provision and profitability, is the most efficient and restrictive manner to protect market share. The emergence of a hub and spoke structure may indicate how the European airline business will respond to a greater degree of deregulation in the 1990s. But as the discussion by Heraty (1989) suggests, the supply of tourist transport services in destination areas needs to be carefully targeted at the market to ensure both customer satisfaction and to maximise revenue generation for private sector transport operators. Yet as the case of Bermuda shows, where there is a significant demand for a destination, government action may be taken to restrict the activities of tour operators and tourists without adversely affecting the tourism industry. Understanding the expectations and motives of visitors reaffirms the importance of setting the demand and supply for tourist transport services in a systematic framework where the wider issues and inter-relationships can be understood. In this context, the next chapter considers the human effects and environmental consequences of tourist travel which are assuming a more prominent position in the tourist's perception and impressions of the transport services they consume.

Questions

1 Evaluate the use of a transaction analysis in understanding the process of supplying tourist transport services.
2 Examine a tourist transport operator's annual report. What operational data and financial information does it contain?
3 What lessons can the North American experience of airline deregulation offer for the EC?
4 What measures do tourist transport operators need to take to ensure that the supply of services meets minimum standards in destination areas?

Further reading

Hodgson, A. (ed.) (1987) *The Travel and Tourism Industry: Strategies for the Future*, Oxford: Pergamon.
Sinclair, M.T. and Stabler, M. (eds) (1991) *The Tourism Industry: An International Analysis*, Wallingford: CAB International.
Thornberry, N. and Hennessey, H. (1992) 'Customer care, much more than a smile: developing a customer-service infrastructure', *European Management Journal* 10, 4: 460–4.
Witt, S.F., Brooke, M.Z.and Buckley, P.J. (1991) *The Management of International Tourism*, London: Unwin Hyman.

6
The human
and environmental
consequences
of tourist transport

Introduction

The international expansion of tourism and the development of transport systems to meet this demand have had a range of direct and indirect social, cultural, economic and physical impacts on both host populations affected by the operation of tourist transport, and destination areas. In the 1970s and 1980s this led to a growing concern for the impact of tourist travel on the environment, but little attention has been given to the experiences for tourists whilst in transit. This chapter examines the effect and impact of tourist transport from two perspectives: the effect of travelling on the tourists' experience and the impact of transport systems on the environment. In Chapters 1 and 2, the concept of the service encounter was discussed (by using Bitner *et al.* 1990) which recognises that satisfaction and dissatisfaction associated with tourism services are associated with three types of incidents: employee failure to respond adequately to customer needs; unprompted and unsolicited employee actions; and service delivery failure (Ryan 1991: 42–3). It is the last which is the focus in the first part of this chapter, particularly how travel delays and service interruptions may contribute to the stress of tourist travel, and some of the measures taken by transport operators to address such problems. This is followed by a discussion of environmental issues from the transport providers' perspective, including the role of environmental auditing and environmental assessment to address the long-term implications of new tourist transport projects on the environment. This is followed by a discussion of the extent to which sustainable tourist travel may assist in identifying ways of reducing transport's impact on the environment.

The human consequences of modern tourist travel

Previous chapters have shown that the tourist travel experience is a complex phenomenon to understand. Social psychologists (Pearce 1982) and marketers are continuously trying to understand the relationship between consumer behaviour (Qaiters and Bergiel 1989; Schiffman and Kanuk 1991) and tourist travel (Goodall 1991), the tourists' degree of satisfaction with travel services and their propensity to revisit destinations in the future. One area which has really lacked serious academic research is the tourists' feelings and the trauma sometimes associated with international travel (a more detailed discussion of tourist health can be found in Clift and Page, forthcoming). In terms of foreign travel, stress is a feature often overlooked since tour operators and travel agents often extol the virtues of taking a holiday to fulfil a deep psychological need (see Chapter 4). Ryan (1991) notes that tourist travel experiences offer many potential avenues of research. The stress associated with international, and to a lesser degree domestic, travel is the result of various psychological factors which are compounded by the effect of congestion on transport systems. McIntosh (1990a) argues that the stress of travel could be attributed to:

- preflight anxieties
- airside problems
- transmeridian disturbance
- fears and phobias
- psychological concerns

while in-flight health problems can also be added to the stress involved in modern-day long-haul travel.

Preflight anxieties emerge when tourists commence their journey, when travelling to the place of departure, often to meet schedules imposed by airlines. McIntosh (1990a: 118) suggests that the marketing of travel insurance to cover eventualities such as missed departures can also heighten the inexperienced traveller's sense of anxiety. Once at the departure point, the preflight check-in and the complex array of security checks associated with luggage can subject the traveller to a significant amount of stress in an unfamiliar environment. Furthermore, 'the apprehension . . . initially generated by preflight security . . . searches . . . [are] . . . a reminder of the risk of hijack and in-flight explosion' (McIntosh 1990a: 118). Overcrowding at peak times in terminal buildings associated with the throughput of passengers can overwhelm and disorientate travellers, while seasoned frequent travellers (e.g. business travellers) often have access to executive lounges and a more relaxed and welcoming environment free from some of these stress-producing factors.

Airside problems, including the design and layout of holding areas for passengers travelling economy class, may contribute to an impersonal and dehumanising process prior to departure which is exacerbated by an absence of information regarding the nature and duration of delays. As Ryan (1991: 43) argues 'passengers delayed in air terminals might be observed as passing through a process of arousal to anxiety, to worry, to apathy, as they become initially frustrated by delays which eventually reaches apathy because of an inability to control events'.

Transmeridian disturbance associated with time zone changes during long-haul travel is a major problem for some travellers. The condition is often associated with a lack of sleep on long-haul flights and a sleep–wake cycle which can cause exhaustion, commonly referred to as 'jet-lag'. The advice of travel agents to some clients may need to be sensitive to the effect of transmeridian disturbance for those suffering from depression. Taking a long-haul holiday to forget their problems may heighten their sense of depression on east–west travel across the world's main time zones.

Fears and phobias associated with the likelihood of political insurrections, how hospitable the host population will be and potential language difficulties in the destination region all contribute to the traveller's existing apprehension in transit. This stress can be alleviated by in-flight entertainment and public relations campaigns by national tourism organisations to reduce travellers' fears. The threat of terrorism or hijack is also an underlying worry for some travellers. Travellers' anxiety appears to follow a cyclical pattern, being heightened after an incident which is followed by public relations exercises by airlines to reassure passengers of the increased security measures which are in place. Yet in extreme cases, terrorism may pose a major threat to travel. For example, terrorist activity and threats in Europe actually deterred North American visitors from travelling to popular destinations such as London in the 1980s.

Psychological concerns, such as loneliness and a sense of isolation, can also contribute to the traveller's feelings of anonymity during their journey, particularly if a tourist is travelling alone. The experience is often heightened on a busy Jumbo jet carrying approximately 500 passengers, where an individual feels a sense of anonymity and of being confined in a strange environment 10,000 m up in the sky. Safety issues also induce a sense of unease among travellers following an incident such as an air crash. Although air crashes are rare occurrences (Steward 1986) in terms of the volume of passengers carried, and the number of take-offs and landings undertaken, they do assume a prominent role in the psychology of tourist travel. In-flight health-related problems may also affect passengers on long-haul flights where immobility, reduced air pressure within the flight cabin and dehydration may occur due to the recirculation of dry air within the aircraft. There is also a growing concern on the effect of smoking on long-haul flights as recirculated air may lead to passive smoking risks when air filters are not adequately maintained. One less common, but nonetheless worrying, feature for health professionals is the role of long-haul aircraft in carrying passengers with infectious diseases during their incubation period (Cossar *et al.* 1990; Reid and Cossar 1993; Mann and Mantel 1992). At the destination, tourists may need reassurance when using local transport systems where operators give the impression of being blasé or unconcerned about safety issues and passenger welfare. There are also a range of other, more persistent, physical problems that affect the tourist's experience in transit, most notably *motion sickness*.

McIntosh (1990b: 80) provides a useful overview of motion sickness as a 'debilitating but relatively short-lived illness which indiscriminately affects air, land and sea travellers'. Yardley (1992) examines the literature associated with the concept of motion sickness, casting doubt over previous explanations of its causes and the tourist's susceptibility. It is clear from the existing literature on travellers' health that this affliction is not fully understood. Some researchers believe it is associated with the way in which different modes of transport stimulate an alteration in the perceived stability of the travel environment (i.e. motion changes – such as swaying from side to side or violent changes in altitude due to turbulence in air travel) and this affects one's sensory system. It may affect the traveller's perception of the environment and cause various symptoms such as drowsiness, vomiting, increased pulse rate, yawning, cold sweats, nausea and impaired digestion. Although some drug therapy may attempt to block the effects of motion sickness, no comprehensive cure exists and McIntosh

(1990b: 82–3) reviews measures to assist the traveller in overcoming sea, car and air sickness.

The experience of travel stress-producing factors and health-related problems may be severe among certain groups such as the elderly. McIntosh (1989) reviews the range of problems which the elderly may experience on tourist transport systems, such as immobility and confusion when a series of time zone changes are crossed during a journey. In view of the increasingly aged structure of tourism markets in developed countries (see Viant 1993), the welfare of elderly travellers and their service experience in transit are assuming a greater significance among the more innovative transport carriers. According to Viant (1993), the 'senior travel market' (those over 55 years of age) in Europe accounts for 20 per cent of domestic and international tourist trips and is forecast to increase from 142.1 million trips in 1990 to 255.2 million by the year 2000, an increase of 79.6 per cent. As growing numbers of senior travellers experience excellent health, it is evident that this niche market will pose many opportunities for the tourist transport system. What measures can transport operators take to reduce the stressful experience associated with different aspects of tourist travel?

- The provision of special assistance at airports for senior travellers and disabled tourists, building on Thomas Cook's innovative Airport Travel Services for group travel to reduce the stress for group organisers taking large parties of tourists abroad.
- The development of 'fear of travelling' programmes for different modes of transport, especially air travel (e.g. Thomson Holidays in the UK offers such a scheme through its own airline Britannia and British Airways also offers a 1 day fear of flying programme).
- Planners and designers can improve the structure and appearance of terminal buildings so that they are built with the customer in mind, by reducing the stress of being in an unfamiliar environment. The award-winning design of the Stansted airport terminal building (London) is one example of how to incorporate these principles into new terminal buildings. This contrasts markedly with smaller '1930s-style' regional airports (e.g. Jersey in the Channel Islands) which have inadequate space to accommodate departing tourists in their check-in area, an absence of air conditioning in the departure area, and too few seats at the departure gates requiring passengers to sit on the floor in the height of the summer season. This was one result of bunching charter flights on a Saturday rather than distributing them

across the week in the 1993 season, which undoubtedly contributes to the stress of tourist travel due to overcrowding and unnecessary queuing induced through poor planning and inadequate staffing levels. It is apparent that many of the first-generation '1930s airports' are now too small and not designed with the 1990s tourist–traveller in mind.

- The provision of accurate and up to date information when travel delays occur.
- Prior to the take-off of an aircraft, the airline staff should inform travellers of the sounds they will hear (e.g. as wheels are retracted and the change in engine sound at the cruising altitude) to allay any fears.
- The provision of accurate in-flight advice for travellers, such as KLM Royal Dutch Airlines' *Comfort in Flight* brochure.
- The introduction of low-profile security checks at ports of departure so that 'anxiety-provoking intensive security screening' (McIntosh 1990a: 120) reduces the potential for passenger stress.
- In extreme cases, General Practitioners may prescribe mild medication (e.g. diazepam) to relax the traveller in-flight, but this is often a last resort.

To date, research on tourists' experience of travel has focused on travellers' health, health precautions prior to departure and problems encountered at the destination (see the journal *Travel Medicine International*). This discussion, however, has shown that throughout the transport system, greater attention needs to be paid to the tourist's experience in transit owing to the range of problems travel may engender. As Gunn (1988: 163) suggests,

tourists seek several personal travel factors and will opt for the best combination . . . [of] comfort (freedom from fatigue, discomfort, poor reliability), convenience (absence of delays, cumbersome systems, roundabout routines), safety (freedom from risk, either from the equipment or other people), dependability (reliable schedules and conditions of travel), price (reasonable, competitive) and speed.

Thus tourist 'transportation is more than movement – it is an experience' (Gunn 1988: 167) which the operator needs to recognise so that the total travel experience is as free from inconvenience and stress as possible. Tourist transport not only has an impact on the traveller, but also affects the environment. For this reason, the second part of the chapter considers some of the issues associated with the environmental effects of tourist transport.

The environmental impact of tourist transport

During the 1980s, there was increasing concern with environmental issues and the impact of different forms of economic development, particularly tourism. This international growth in *environmentalism* has meant that there is a greater emphasis on the protection, conservation and management of the environment as a natural and finite resource. Within the tourism and transport business, this concern has emerged in the form of the concept of *sustainable* tourism which highlights the vulnerability of the environment to human impacts from tourism and the need to consider its long-term maintenance. Much of the work on sustainability can be dated to the influential 1987 World Commission on Environment and Development report 'Our Common Future' (Bründt-land 1987) which notes that 'we have not inherited the earth from our parents but borrowed it from our children'. In other words, sustainable development is based on the principle of 'meeting the needs of the present without compromising the ability of future generations to meet their own needs' (Bründtland 1987) which requires some understanding of the natural environment's ability to sustain certain types of economic activities such as transport and tourism. However, research on transport and tourism has often been considered in isolation, as the following discussion will show, although the use of research techniques such as environmental auditing and environmental assessment may assist in bridging this gap, to recognise the specific impacts induced by tourist transport systems.

Transport and the environment

Within the context of tourist transport systems, transport features as one component of a much wider concern for more sustainable forms of development as the problems relating to the impact of transport on the environment are symptomatic of the need for more environmentally sensitive forms of development. Within the context of transport planning, there has also been a greater understanding of the complex and sometimes detrimental impact of certain forms of transport on the environment. The emerging environmental research on the impact of different modes of transport (TEST 1991), has focused on the implications, for transport and policy-making (Department of the Environment 1991), in relation to controversial new tourist and non-tourist infrastructure projects. This interest in the impact of infra-structure projects has led to measures for environmental mitigation. The emphasis on the environment has also led to detailed research on specific components of environmental problems induced by transport such as:

- health and safety
- air pollution
- noise pollution
- ecological impacts
- the environmental effects of different modes of transport

One consequence of such research is that policy-makers have focused on the direct costs and problems associated with the development of new transport infrastructure, which is now subject to more rigorous environmental safeguards to minimise the detrimental impacts. This concern for the environmental dimension has also been mirrored in tourism research.

Tourism and the environment

As discussed in Chapter 2, the increasing sophistication among tourists has been reflected in the development of a 'new tourism' (Poon 1989), accompanied by a greater emphasis on the consumer requirements of tourists in terms of their search for more authentic holiday experiences and individualised tourism services. One consequence of this 'new tourism' phenomenon is a greater concern for the natural and built environment in which tourism activities are undertaken and its impact in different localities. This greater awareness of environmental issues related to tourism is reflected in the rapid expansion and diversity of research on 'sustainable tourism' (Smith and Eadington 1992), which emphasises the need for a more holistic assessment of how tourist-related activities (e.g. tourist transport) affect the environment.

Recent reviews of research on the environmental dimension in tour-ism have identified the scope and nature of this growing body of knowledge as well as the existing weaknesses in the structure and form of such studies (Pearce 1985). The recognition of the symbiotic relation-ship between conservation and tourism (Romeril 1985) has led to the need for a greater integration of interdisciplinary and multidisciplinary approaches to research on tourism and the environment to achieve sustainable tourism development, of which transport is an integral component. This focuses on the need to overcome tourism's tendency sometimes to destroy the very resources it depends upon. This very objective is the focus of the recent 'Tourism and the Environment Report' (English Tourist Board/Employment Department 1991) aimed at encouraging the UK tourism industry to recognise that the environment is its very lifeblood and that it needs to consider the long-term consequences of tourism activity and development. Although Romeril (1989) argues that this mutual dependence of tourism and the environment requires appropriate strategies and methodologies to understand the complex inter-relationships between the interaction of tourism and the environment, no universal environmental methodology appears to have been adopted by researchers in their assessment of tourism and the role of transport in affecting the environment.

It is evident from the discussion so far that tourism and tourist transport systems are consumers of the environment (Goodall 1992) since the provision of tourist infrastructure has a direct impact on the environment, particularly in destination areas. Selman (1992) and Newson (1992) discuss the concept of environmental auditing as one way of examining the extent to which tourist transport systems and their activities are environmentally acceptable. Does tourist transport cause unnecessary pollution? Can measures be taken to mitigate and reduce the harmful effects on the environment without compromising the commercial objectives of the tourist transport operator? According to Goodall (1992: 62) one needs to distinguish between two types of environmental concern:

- the existing impacts of tourist transport
- the future impacts of tourist transport.

Here two types of research methodology can be used:

- Environmental auditing of existing transport systems and their performance and effect on the natural and built environment.
- Environmental assessment to consider the impact of proposed developments in the tourist transport system.

Each methodology has been developed as a multidisciplinary technique requiring an input from disciplines such as economics, atmospheric science, environmental science, geography, management studies and planning. Within these techniques, a systems approach is often used as a method of examining how different tourist transport inputs affect the environment, and how to mitigate the effects of outputs which contribute to environmental degradation (Wathern 1990).

Environmental auditing and tourist transport

Within tourism and transport studies the two most notable studies published on environmental auditing (e.g. Goodall 1992 and Sommerville 1992) illustrate how this research technique is used as a response to the growing interest in sustainable development (Banister and Button 1992). Environmental auditing is a voluntary exercise which tourist transport operators and tour operators, who contract transport services for clients, may undertake to assess how their activities affect the environment and ways of reducing the impact by making modifications to existing business practices. Newson (1992: 100) notes that 'the term auditing, borrowed from finance, implies a thoroughness and openness which is essential in a meaningful desire to reform commercial practices' but few environmental audits have been publicised. Some examples from the field of consumer products (e.g. the Body Shop and Proctor and Gamble in the UK) have followed the lead of North America in terms of consumer demand for more 'green products' (Selman 1992). Critics argue that such new found environmental awareness by companies has been harnessed to gain competitive advantage by increasing market share by offering environmentally friendly services and products as part of the move towards total quality management within their organisation. Even so, committed transport operators who undertake an environmental audit may prompt other companies to follow suit, thereby improving the awareness of environmental issues within their sector of the tourism business. The recent establishment of the British Standards Institution's (BSI) new Environmental Management System, mirroring the BS 5750 quality system for service providers, is evidence of the significance of environmental auditing as a potent force in the 1990s which will encourage companies to establish a benchmark of acceptable standards of environmental management in commercial activities. Tourist-transport systems are no exception to this environmental awareness and it is likely to increase in the 1990s. For example, at the time of writing, P & O European Ferries had undertaken a comprehensive environmental review and are implementing environmental policies to reduce the company's impact on the atmosphere, marine environment and on-shore.

Goodall (1992) identifies the place of environmental auditing in corporate policy-making among tourism enterprises (e.g. transport providers) which includes:

- *a consideration stage*, where the legislation and scope of environmental issues are considered
- *a formulation stage*, where an environmental policy is developed
- *an implementation stage*, where both existing and proposed activities can be considered
- *a decision stage*, where transport operations are either modified or left unchanged in pursuit of a corporate environmental policy.

More specifically, Goodall (1992: 64) recognises that policy statements and action to minimise environmental impacts need to consider:

- the extent to which transport operations and associated activities comply with environmental legislation through company regulations
- ways of reducing negative environmental impacts such as polluting emissions and use of energy-efficient modes of transport and equipment based on state-of-the-art technology
- the development of 'environmentally friendly' products
- encouraging a greater understanding of environmental issues among staff, customers and people affected by tourist transport.

Translating these principles into commercial practice is a complex process even though organisations such as the World Travel and Tourism Council recommended that such audits should be undertaken annually to foster more responsible forms of development (Goodall 1992). As Table 6.1 shows, the nature and scope of environmental auditing in the tourist transport system may be determined by the objectives, commitment of senior management, and the size of their organisation to resource such an exercise. One tourist transport operator which has developed a corporate audit is British Airways.

Case study 9: British Airways and environmental management

Consumer interest in environmental issues in the late 1980s prompted tourist transport operators in the UK (e.g. P & O European Ferries, British Airways and BR) to undertake environmental

Case study 9 (*continued*)

Table 6.1 Types of environmental audit

Audit	
Activity	An overview of an activity or process which crosses business boundaries in a company, e.g. staff travel by employees of a hotel chain.
Associate	Auditing of firms which act as agents, subcontractors or suppliers of inputs, e.g. tour operators using only hotels which have adequate waste water and sewage treatment or disposal facilities and which are in keeping with the character of a destination.
Compliance	Relatively simple, regular checks to ensure the firm complies with any current environmental regulations affecting its operations, e.g. airline checking on noise levels of its aircraft at take-off.
Corporate	Typically an audit of an entire company, especially a transnational one, to ensure that agreed environmental policy is understood and followed throughout the firm.
Issues	Concentration upon a key issue, e.g. ozone depletion, and evaluation of company operations in relation to that issue, e.g. hotel chain checks aerosols used are CFC free, uses only alternatives to CFC-blown plastic foams for insulation and retrieves any CFCs used in air-conditioning plant for controlled disposal.
Product	Ensuring that existing products and proposed product developments meet the firm's environmental policy criteria, e.g. tour operator designs holiday based on walking once destination reached, using locally owned vernacular accommodation and services.
Site	Audit directed at spot checks of buildings, plant and processes known to have actual or potential problems, e.g. hotel checking energy efficiency of its heating and lighting systems, airport authority checking aircraft noise levels near to landing and take-off flight paths.

Source: Goodall (1992: 68).

audits to provide a public image of 'environmentally conscious' companies. Purchasers of tourist transport services (e.g. tour operators such as Thomson Holidays) also undertook environmental audits to respond to this trend. This case study focuses on the extent of environmental management by one of the world's largest

Case study 9 (*continued*)

tourist transport operators – British Airways. The significance of British Airways (hereafter BA) as a tourist transport company has been documented elsewhere (see Laws 1991) and need not be reiterated here. Commercial aviation dominates the world's communications infrastructure since over '8800 subsonic jet aircraft . . . flew over 1.7 billion passenger kilometres in 1990' (Sommerville 1992: 161). BA's role in the world airline industry is reflected in its $9 billion turnover in 1990–1, having carried 25 million passengers on its fleet of 230 aircraft (Sommerville 1992). Air travel is also a useful example to focus on in relation to its impact on the environment as a variety of impacts arise from airline operation which can be dealt with under the following headings:

Noise Early tourist travel on the early turbo-prop and jet-propelled aircraft generated a significant noise impact during take-off, in-flight and on landing (see Farrington 1992 for a discussion of the technical issues). Modern aircraft technology has reduced the level of noise impact since international conventions and legal requirements at specific airports aim to reduce noise impacts for local communities. But the sheer volume of air travel creates a persistent problem for those affected by the airline's flight path. As Sommerville (1992) notes, since the 1970s the number of people affected by noise nuisance at Heathrow within a 35 Noise Index Number Contour has dropped by almost 75 per cent, but this was accompanied by a dramatic increase in the volume of air travel. Increasingly airports are monitoring individual aircraft (e.g. their noise footprint) to ensure they meet noise regulations (see M.J.T. Smith 1989 for further information). The phasing out of older aircraft is one way of reducing the noise impact in line with recent guidelines issued by countries abiding by ICAO recommendations. From April 1995, aircraft over 25 years old are to be replaced in countries abiding by ICAO guidelines while additional regulations will apply in European airspace. BA's (1992) 'Annual Environmental Report' lists its fleet composition and its plans to replace its older 'Chapter 2' aircraft (e.g. BAC 1-11-500s) (see Table 6.2) in advance of the ICAO guidelines. In 1990–1,

Table 6.2 British Airways fleet composition, as at 31 March 1992 (including Caledonian Airways Ltd, but not Gibraltar Airways)

Aircraft type	Engine type	ICAO Annex 16 Chapter/FAR Part 36 Stage	London Airport's night noise category landing/take-off	Number of aircraft	Average age of aircraft (years)
Concorde	Olympus 593	Exempt	Exempt	7	15.3
Boeing 747-100	JT9D 7/7A	2	NNB/NNB	15	19.9
Boeing 747-200	RB211-524D4X	3	NNB/NNB	16	11.3
Boeing 747-400	RB211-524G/H2	3	NNB/NNB	22	1.8
Lockheed Tristar 1, 50, 100	RB211-22B	3	NNB/NNB	6	17.0
McDonnell Douglas DC 10-30	CF6-50C2	3	NNB/NNB	8	13.3
Boeing 767-300	RB211-524H	3	NNC/NNC	16	1.5
Boeing 757-200	RB211-535C/E4	3	NNC/NNC	37	6.2
Airbus A320 100/200	CFM56-5A1	3	NNC/NNC	10	3.1
Boeing 737-200	JT8D-15A	2	NNB/NNB	41	10.1
Boeing 737-400	CFM56-3C1	3	NNC/NNC	13	0.3
BAC 1-11-500	SPEY 514 DW	2	NNB/NNA	24	23.6
BAe ATP	PW126	5/Stage 3	Exempt	13	2.0
HS 748-2B	DART 536-2	Exempt	Exempt	2	16.4
TOTAL				230	10.1

Source: British Airways (1992: 6).

Case study 9 (*continued*)

Table 6.3 Airline emissions

| Emission | Environmental effects | Approximate emissions (millions of tonnes) | |
		Commercial aviation	Worldwide (fossil fuels)
Oxides of nitrogen	Acid rain; ozone formation at cruise altitudes and smog and ozone at low levels	0.6	69[1]
Hydrocarbons	Ozone and smog formation at low levels	0.4	57[1]
Carbon monoxide	Toxic	0.9	193[1]
Carbon dioxide	Stable – contributes to Greenhouse effect by absorption and reflection of infrared radiation	500–600	20,000[1]
Sulphur dioxide	Acid rain	1.1	110[1]
Water vapour	Greenhouse effect by absorption and reflection of infrared radiation	200–300	7,900[2]
Smoke	Nuisance – effects depend on composition	Negligible	n/a

Notes:
1 OECD Secretariat estimates (for 1980), from OECD Environmental Data 1989.
2 Derived from BP Statistical Review of Energy, 1991.

Aviation figures from AEA estimates apart from NO_x.

Other emissions, mainly from paints and cleaning solvents, are associated with aircraft maintenance and also from ground transport supporting the airline's operation.

Source: British Airways (1992: 8).

BA was charged £3 million by airports for noise pollution from the use of Chapter 2 aircraft (e.g. 747-100s, 747-200s and BAC 1-11-500s), which provided a commercial incentive to phase out ageing aircraft. BA has also undertaken research in conjunction with the Civil Aviation Authority (CAA), Department of Transport and the local community near Heathrow to assess whether people's sleep pattern at night is disturbed by night-flying.

Case study 9 (*continued*)

Emissions and fuel efficiency   The growing concern over global warming and 'greenhouse gases' (e.g. CFCs, CO_2, NO_x and methane) has meant that atmospheric pollution from aircraft has come under increasing scrutiny. BA (1992) identified the range of emissions from aviation (Table 6.3) and quantified its own emissions in the air based on the consumption of 3,560,000 million tonnes of fuel in 1990–1. This resulted in the:

• use of 4,960,000 tonnes of water
• production of 15,700 tonnes of carbon monoxide
• generation of 40,200 tonnes of nitrogen oxide
• production of 21,300 tonnes of sulphur dioxide.

On the ground, emissions may affect local air quality, though BA argued that this is minimal compared with the contribution from cars, taxis, bus and freight transport using airports. BA estimates that from its ground operations in 1990–1 the following emissions occurred:

• 630 tonnes of hydrocarbons
• 20,000 tonnes of carbon dioxide.

Waste water, energy and materials   In 1990, BA's expenditure on waste disposal was £1.5 million and it has pursued a corporate 'reduce, reuse and recycle' philosophy. Recycling of aircraft materials (e.g. waste oil, tyres, batteries and metals) has been in place ince the 1950s and aluminium and paper recycling occurs, while water and effluent management schemes have been reviewed to ensure the quality of the waste is improved. Complex energy efficiency monitoring is also undertaken to identify energy savings. BA's use of CFCs and chlorocarbon (CC) in its engineering operations for cleaning purposes has been reviewed and alternatives are being sought, with aerosol use replaced wherever possible by trigger sprays. De-icing fluid used in its airport operations is biodegradable and there is evidence of a decline in its use between 1989 and 1991.

Case study 9 (*continued*)

Congestion   Congestion is viewed by BA as 'the most immediate problem facing the aviation industry in Europe. It is estimated that delays in the air and on the ground cost the industry some $5 billion per year . . . and could rise to $10 billion per year by 2000' (BA 1992: 22). Congestion increases fuel consumption, resulting in additional emissions, particularly where a lack of airspace, air traffic control problems and inadequate runway capacity delay flights. BA estimates that air traffic delays led to the consumption of an additional 60,000 tonnes of fuel at Heathrow and Gatwick in 1990–1. This is accentuated by taxiing delays prior to take-off and after landing where an additional 21,600 tonnes of fuel were consumed by BA's aircraft. Measures to improve airport capacity at Heathrow with the proposed Terminal 5 and the use of larger aircraft may assist in reducing congestion, although the CAA has constantly emphasised the need for an additional runway in SE England by 2005 to address congestion issues. But an additional runway may lead to increased environmental impacts in terms of the landtake and effect on the local community.

Tourism   BA (1992) acknowledges that the environmental impact created by tourists travelling on aircraft to destinations is an issue which falls under the remit of its environmental management programme. BA perceives its role as one of environmental education by (BA 1992: 25):

- raising awareness of the (environmental) issues within the industry and with customers
- persuading governments and tourist authorities to impose discipline and appropriate planning regulations and management procedures to ensure future tourist development is managed in an environmentally responsible way.

So how can one evaluate BA's performance in the environmental management of tourist transport?

One initial issue to consider is BA's stated environmental policy which is reproduced in Table 6.4. This illustrates an integrated approach to environmental management so that the company

Case study 9 (*continued*)

Table 6.4 British Airways environmental policy

Mission – Environment Branch

To promote throughout the airline policies and actions that shall benefit the environment and that shall inspire the confidence of our customers, our staff and the public alike.

Goals

The Environment Branch seeks to influence departments and staff throughout British Airways:

• To develop awareness and understanding of the interactions between the airline's operations and the environment.
• To maintain a healthy working environment for all our employees.
• To consider and respect the environment and to seek to protect the environment in the course of their activities.

Environment strategy

British Airways will strive to achieve these goals by:

• Taking account of environment issues in our commercial decision-making.
• Working constructively with organisations concerned for the environment.
• Promoting our environmental activities with our staff and customers and letting them know of our concern and care for the environment.
• Observing rules and regulations aimed at protecting the environment.
• Providing support and advice on environmental matters relating to our operations.
• Using natural resources efficiently.

Source: British Airways (1992).

---

complies with all existing environmental regulations. It also highlights the corporate ethos – to ensure 'all staff are responsible for safeguarding, as far as they are able, both their working environment and the greater environment surrounding [their] operations' (BA 1992: 30). To encourage a greater environmental awareness within and outside the organisation BA has established a number of initiatives:

Within the organisation:

• a network of 'Environmental Champions' has been established to promote environmental activity in different departments

Case study 9 (*continued*)

- market research has been undertaken on the environmental issues related to airline operations
- 'Greenseal Awards' have been introduced as corporate awards for excellence for environmental achievements and a 'Greenwaves' scheme implemented to encourage environmental suggestions from staff
- the promotion of staff awareness of environmental issues in company publications and in a quarterly environmental newsletter.

Outside of the organisation:

- funding of the World Travel and Tourism World Environment Centre at Oxford Brookes University
- sponsorship of the television 'Wish You Were Here?' holiday programme 'Tourism for Tomorrow' awards
- nature conservation measures, including BA's 'Assisting Nature Conservation' to assist in education, training and natural habitat management and protection.

In evaluating the scope of BA's environmental measures, it is evident that the organisation is establishing a benchmark by 'taking the lead [but] it is up to other sectors of the industry to extend the initiative' (Sommerville 1992: 173).

Environmental researchers have also developed a greater interest in the future impact of tourist transport systems in terms of the requirement for additional infrastructure and its impact on the environment, which is now considered in relation to environmental assessment.

Environmental assessment and tourist transport

An understanding of the past and present effect of tourist transport systems on the environment is critical to the long-term management of environmental resources, but there is also a need to consider the likely effect of future transport development projects. It is within this context that the significance of research methodologies such as environmental assessment (EA) can be examined to show how future tourist transport infrastructure projects may be evaluated. Within the existing literature on the environmental impact of tourism and transport, a number of research methodologies exist, which are documented by Williams (1987) in terms of their analytical function and the techniques they employ. There are three levels at which EA of tourism and transport projects can be undertaken: 'identification', 'prediction' and 'evaluation'. Williams (1987) summarises five main methodologies used to assess the impact of tourism on the environment in which transport is a significant component. These range from *ad hoc* teams of specialists describing impacts within their professional field of study, to the 'map overlay approach' frequently used in land use planning, through to 'check-lists' of different impacts associated with physical development related to tourism, 'networks' to assess the secondary and tertiary effects associated with action relating to tourism projects, and lastly, more sophisticated matrices of impacts within the confines of EA (see Wathern 1990 for a more detailed discussion). Although EA was not specifically designed with tourist transport projects in mind, it is a useful methodological tool to examine the direct and indirect effect of a project on the existing and future tourism environment within an integrated research framework (see Department of the Environment 1989 for a guide to the scope and complex range of issues which EA in the UK must address as a legal requirement). To illustrate how an EA has considered a tourist transport system and some of its potential shortcomings (see Ross 1987 for a discussion of how to evaluate EAs), the case of the Channel Tunnel is now examined.

Case study 10: The environmental impact of a new tourist transport infrastructure project – the Channel Tunnel

The Channel Tunnel is currently the largest tourist transport infrastructure project in Europe, expected to cost in excess of £10 billion. According to SERPLAN (1989), the Channel Tunnel could generate an additional 450,000 tourists for the south east of England in 1993 who will use various modes of transport to travel through the tunnel to mainland Europe. Whilst not wishing to reiterate the issues discussed in Chapter 2, it is evident that the

Case study 10 (*continued*)

tunnel project will create a new tourist gateway between the United Kingdom and mainland Europe, thereby facilitating more choice in the available modes of cross-Channel travel for tourists after 1993. The extent to which the opening of the Channel Tunnel will directly and indirectly affect physical and man-made tourism environments in the 1990s is largely overlooked in recent research on the Channel Tunnel (Page 1994).

The environmental dimension has not received a great deal of attention, with the exception of the controversy related to the routing of the Channel Tunnel high-speed rail link through Kent (see Goodenough and Page 1994). In the UK, the environmental lobby is particularly concerned with the physical impact, although the majority of such studies have focused on a specific impact rather than the tunnel's effect in different tourism environments in the 1990s.

Environmental assessment and the Channel Tunnel

In the UK the EC Directive (85/337/EEC) on EA coincided with the government's 'Invitation to Promoters for the Development, Financing, Construction and Operation of a Channel Fixed Link between France and the United Kingdom'. Wathern (1990) examines the recalcitrance of certain member states, particularly the UK, towards adopting the Directive since the government's commitment to push the Channel Tunnel project to fruition as quickly as possible in 1985. By using the parliamentary device of the Hybrid Bill, no public planning enquiry was needed which avoided any obligatory participation in an EA to comply with the impending EC legislation since 'the Directive does not apply to projects . . . which are authorised by a private or Hybrid Bill' (Department of the Environment 1989: 23), although 'the promoter of such a Bill should provide an environmental statement which can be considered by the select or standing committees . . . on the Bill' (Department of the Environment 1989: 23). The latter situation applied to the four shortlisted promoters of the Fixed Link project (Channel Tunnel Group, Channel Expressway, Eurobridge and

Case study 10 (*continued*)

Euroroute) who were required to comply with the EC Directive in 1985. This meant that rather than preparing a simple environmental statement, a detailed EA was required from each promoter, minimising the cost to the government by requiring the private sector to fund a detailed environmental analysis. As a result, the EAs of the Fixed Link project are a landmark in the UK since they were the first to comply with the EC Directive 85/337.

The four shortlisted promoters' EA reports submitted in 1985 were subsequently appraised by Land Use Consultants (1986) who reviewed the content, coverage, accuracy and presentation of the reports in relation to their ability to meet the requirements of the EC Directive 85/337. Evaluating EAs is a complex process in view of the problems of understanding and forecasting the secondary effects and consequential development such projects may generate. For example, the Channel Tunnel Group's EA (Channel Tunnel Group 1985) underestimated the potential impact of a new mode of new tourist transport on tourism, arguing that the tunnel in itself would not directly stimulate a growth in the demand for cross-Channel travel. Yet this overlooks the new tourism markets which will be made more accessible to the UK and Europe by the tunnel and improvements to the high-speed European rail network and roads (Page and Sinclair 1992b; Page 1993e). Thus, while the Channel Tunnel Group's EA dealt with the physical impacts involved with construction of the tunnel it failed to make a detailed assessment of the consequences of a growth in visitor arrivals induced by the Fixed Link. Criticisms of the Channel Tunnel Group's EA have also pointed to the voluminous and unintelligible nature of the study (Lee and Wood 1988). Although the EA failed to consider the potential environmental impacts associated with a sustained growth in visitor arrivals and departures once the tunnel opened, it is possible to identify a number of ways in which tourist use of the tunnel will affect the environment:

The environmental impact of constructing the tunnel on existing tourism resources   The construction of the tunnel has aroused the concerns of amenity bodies such as the Council for the Protection

Case study 10 (*continued*)

of Rural England and the Nature Conservancy Council. Ardill (1987) examines the conservation lobby's concern for the impact on the landscape, and the land damaged or lost in the process of constructing the tunnel, the terminals and associated infrastructure, the effects of consequential development on the south east resulting from selective land releases for tourism or motorway service area provision at interchanges. The visual amenity of the Kent landscape will also be affected by the tunnel and tourism resources may be affected by consequential development. The Channel Tunnel Joint Consultative Committee (1986) argues that only a limited environmental impact would result from consequential development associated with the tunnel, based on the fact that since 1970 there has been a three-fold growth in the demand for cross-Channel travel but this has not generated any consequential development or led to any dramatic change in the county's economic geography.

Tourist use of the tunnel and the potential effects on the environment   According to Land Use Consultants (1986: 49) the tunnel could affect tourism in terms of employment and induced development but tourism and recreation would need to be controlled and managed to reduce their impact on the environment. Their general assessment is important in terms of the scale of the potential impact of tourism in relation to how many tourists will travel through the tunnel once it is open. According to SETEC (1989), the traffic-forecasting consultants to Eurotunnel, in 1993 they expect 15.8 million road-borne passengers to travel through the tunnel via the shuttle service. This will virtually double the capacity for crossings after 1993 and the potential environmental impacts largely depend on the extent to which demand grows to fill this increased capacity and the degree of market capture by Eurotunnel of existing ferry and air traffic. This raises the question of how tourist use of the tunnel can be accommodated within the existing environment and the cumulative effects of additional tourists travelling through Kent after 1993.

Case study 10 (*continued*)

Table 6.5 A comparison of pollution from the TGV and car-borne traffic using the motorway in Belgium[1]

Pollutant	TGV *(g/km travelled)*	Car *(g/km travelled)*
Sulphur dioxide[2]	0.124	0.090
Nitrous oxide[3]	0.071	1.460
Aerosol	0.044	0.049
Carbon monoxide[4]	0.005	1.109
Hydrocarbons[5]	0.002	0.179
Carbon dioxide[6]	228.907	135.000
Safety:		
Number of persons killed per billion km travelled	0.8 (train)	20.0 (roads)
	0 (French TGV)	6.7 (motorway)

Notes:
1 The accuracy of the pollution measurements listed in the table will depend on the meteorological conditions and prevailing winds as to whether pollutants concentrate at particular locations or disperse over a wider area.
2 Sulphur dioxide may impair health and it contributes to acid rain as sulphuric acid.
3 Nitrous oxide is a major component in photochemical smog and nitric acid contributes to acid rain. The major emission source is motor vehicles and power stations.
4 Carbon monoxide directly causes health-related problems and it can induce complications among people suffering from cardiac-related diseases. Concentrations of carbon monoxide in confined areas are harmful as it can reduce the oxygen-carrying capacity of the blood.
5 Partially burnt hydrocarbons are carcinogenic (cancer-forming) agents and they also contribute to photochemical smog.
6 Carbon dioxide contributes to the 'Greenhouse effect'.

Source: Cited in Page (1992c) – based on CEDRE (1990).

Direct environmental costs associated with tunnel-related tourist transport infrastructure   The actual impact of major road and rail infrastructure to serve tunnel traffic was assessed within Belgium as part of their EA for the proposed high-speed TGV link from Lille to Brussels. This examines some of the real environmental costs of both road and rail travel by tourists and non-tourists. The purpose of the EA by the European Centre of Regional Development of the Walloon Region (CEDRE 1990) was to assess the 'micro-ecological effects' – the environment in which the infrastructure is to be established. The 'micro-ecological effects' are of interest in this context since they considered the:

Case study 10 (*continued*)

- abiotic impact (e.g. the effect on geology, hydrology, noise and vibration)
- the biological impact (e.g. the effect on flora, fauna and the interactions between the two)
- the human impact (e.g. the effect on agriculture, residential areas, traffic, transport and the human elements in the landscape).

Their assessment of pollution reveals the potential impact tourist travel may have on the environment through which tourists travel – in this case a dedicated transport corridor (Table 6.5). Tourist travel by rail and road produces pollutants, though on balance rail is considered to be the most 'environmentally friendly option', as it is more energy efficient and less intrusive, though it still generates a degree of noise pollution.

The environmental costs and benefits of tourist use of the international passenger terminals Visitors using the Channel Tunnel who travel by rail or road will also generate an environmental impact on their destinations. In the case of London, this impact will largely be related to the IPT at Waterloo (Page and Sinclair 1992a). In Kent, many of the direct environmental impacts will occur at the tunnel terminal and at the planned Ashford IPT, which is likely to be the focus for rail- and car-borne travellers from the south east wishing to board the Eurostar rail services. The environmental impact of increased tourist traffic in Ashford town centre and the proposed construction of the Ashford IPT may transform the town into a rail gateway to Europe. Consultants for BR identify a problem of potential congestion in and around Ashford town centre related to traffic generated by the IPT, which is likely to intensify in view of the predicted 45 per cent growth (1990–2006) in rail travel from Ashford to London and European destinations. The provision of car parking and congestion may concentrate the environmental problems, especially pollution, in a small area of the town, and forecasts' demand for 5,000 car parking spaces in the town illustrates the scale of the IPT development.

Case study 10 (*continued*)

The indirect environmental impact of increased numbers of car-borne tourists on tourist destinations   An associated problem relates to additional car-borne visitors who may stop off in Ashford *en route* to the tunnel for leisure shopping and accommodation, adding to the potential congestion. Although Ashford is unlikely to suffer what Romeril (1989) calls 'saturation tourism' (e.g. seasonally induced peaks in flows of tourists), it is evident that planned visitor management strategies will not be able to overcome all of the problems, particularly once the tunnel is open. The tourism-carrying capacity in Kentish towns like Canterbury has reached saturation point in the peak season (Page 1992b). However, the tunnel will certainly generate the potential for more tourist visits to the county of Kent after 1993; assessing where, when, and the duration of these visits among domestic and overseas tourists likely to use the Fixed Link remains a difficult process. Whatever locations the potential tourists visit, the existing environmental pressures posed by tourist travel to certain destinations in south east England are unlikely to be reduced without some attempts to spread the seasonal distribution of visitors.

The potential problems resulting from the development of a new tourist transport infrastructure project and the implications for destination areas highlight the significance of focusing on the ability of tourist transport to be developed and managed in a sustainable framework.

Towards sustainable tourist transport systems

As mentioned earlier, 'sustainability' is a new found term within the tourism and transportation literature: for services to be attractive to consumers they must now be 'sustainable' or 'green', though much of the rhetoric associated with sustainability has not led to radical changes in the operation and management of tourist transport systems – merely some readjustment to accommodate green issues in most cases. As transport is fundamental to tourist travel, some researchers argue that it is not possible to make tourism sustainable without a fundamental revision of the concept of tourism, holidaymaking and the role of travel in modern society. Therefore, without a re-evaluation of pleasure travel, measures designed to introduce sustainability into the tourist transport environment debate are unlikely to address the root cause of the problem: the demand for tourism. Yet since this is unlikely to be influenced in the short term, the immediate issue is to address the environmental impact of existing tourist travel.

The motivation to achieve sustainable tourist travel has resulted from the actions of pressure groups (e.g. Greenpeace, Friends of the Earth and Transport 2000 in the UK), and their views have permeated national governments as such groups have harnessed grassroots pressure from consumers to develop a greener economy and improve the quality of the environment. But it is at government level that commitment needs to be made to formulate, implement and resource policies to facilitate sustainable transport options. In the case of tourist transport systems, little attention is given to this issue as it is often subsumed under the general theme of transport, which has a bias towards domestic concerns and the effect on economic development. The UK Tourism Society's response to the Government Task Force on tourism and the environment (English Tourist Board/Employment Department 1991) suggests that:

> no analysis of the relationship between tourism and the environment can ignore transportation. Tourism is inconceivable without it. Throughout Europe some 40% of leisure time away from home is spent travelling, and the vast majority of this is by car . . . Approaching 30 per cent of the UK's energy requirements go on transportation . . . [and] . . . the impact of traffic congestion, noise and air pollution . . . [will] . . . diminish the quality of the experience for visitors.
>
> (Tourism Society 1990)

How can the sustainability concept be incorporated into the tourist transport system? According to Barbier (1988: 19, cited in Newson 1992), sustainability needs to be viewed as a process in terms of how different systems interact as:

> the wider objective of sustainable economic development is to find the optimal level of interaction among three systems – the biological and resource system, the economic system and the social system, through a dynamic and adaptive process of trade offs.

This means that economic activity, such as tourism, must try to achieve a balance with the natural environment so that the environment can support the activity without generating unacceptable impacts which affect the future resource base. To achieve this objective, the concept of sustainability needs to be built into the operation of tourist transport systems, and the following action is needed in terms of policy-making and management:

- policy formulation
- policy implementation
- facilitating good practice in tourist transport
- the evaluation of sustainable transport practices.

A systems approach is useful in this context as it helps one to understand how the decision-making process associated with the regulation, organisation and management of tourist transport systems (see Chapter 3) affects different elements within the system. In terms of the sustainability concept, actions in one part of the system (e.g. policy formulation) will have repercussions for other parts of the system.

Policy formulation for sustainable tourist transport

Banister and Button (1992: 2) recognise that the 'whole question of sustainable development . . . is – and likely to remain – a central concern of policy-makers and transport is but one element of this'. The rapid growth in long-distance passenger transport and its dominance by aviation at the international scale and the rapid expansion in car ownership within countries pose many problems for policy-makers in attempting to pursue sustainable transport options. And the underlying demand for travel seems set to continue to expand as forecasts for the year 2000 suggest (Edwards 1992). The social and psychological demand for travel and holidays remains a potent force in developed countries. One result of the sustainable debate for policy-makers is that the environmental impact of transport is not just a local issue: it is also a global problem as the case study of BA indicated. This is confirmed by Banister and Button (1992: 5) who argue that 'transport is an important contributor [to the sustainable development debate] at three levels (local, transboundary and global)'. Therefore policy formulation needs to be undertaken in a context where national governments develop transport policies and co-ordinate their responses at transnational and global level through agencies such as the United Nations.

But political commitment to formulating sustainable transport policies at national level may not be compatible with other political priorities. For example, many governments have facilitated the development of tourist transport infrastructure to foster regional tourism development (e.g. Ireland) and to encourage outbound travel (e.g. Japan). Sustainable transport policies may require a re-evaluation of these national transport policy objectives in relation to tourism, transport and the cost to the environment. In the context of the UK (see Banister 1992 for a discussion of national transport policies in the UK), Hall (1993) argues that sustainable transport is neglected from policy-making since the government's White Paper, 'This Common Inheritance' (Department of the Environment 1991) and accompanying policies have paid little attention to transport and the environment. Hall (1993) suggests that a general environmental transport strategy needs to be formulated for the UK (see Table 6.6). Although tourist transport is subsumed within the wider consideration of transport systems in Table 6.6, it does suggest that co-ordinated action is needed in relation to:

• regulatory mechanisms (e.g. by setting a ceiling for emissions)
• financial mechanisms (e.g. incentives to favour energy-efficient modes of travel)
• the introduction of technological advances in transport to encourage the use of more fuel-efficient engines
• the development of an integrated and co-ordinated planning response to transport where land use and transport planning should minimise the distance to travel for economic and leisure activities (e.g. work and shopping).

How does this affect international tourist travel? It would appear that the likely outcome of Hall's (1993) strategy would be the promotion of environmentally friendly modes of travel for tourists. Yet the real issue of existing tourists' travel habits is absent from the policy objectives as it is often perceived as an international problem rather than one nation's sole responsibility.

Implementation of sustainable tourist transport policies

A useful range of government transport policy responses to sustainability issues are discussed in Banister and Button (1992) and one recurrent theme is the need to adopt economic policies to price transport activities so that they reflect the environmental cost. One approach

Table 6.6 Possible components of a strategic, integrated approach to transport planning and investment, at various organisational levels

National/European:

- A new integrated approach to transport planning in which the case for rail investment is evaluated on a basis comparable with that for roads, taking into account the full environmental costs and benefits.
- Within the framework of this integrated approach, the preparation of a long-term expansion plan for rail, with the aim of at least doubling passenger kilometres carried (restoring the situation to that which applied pre-Beeching), increasing substantially rail's share of freight transport, both internationally and domestically, and in general exploiting fully the potential benefits of the Channel Tunnel link to Europe.

The region/county:

- Through land use planning at the regional and/or county level, the maintenance of an appropriate balance of homes and employment to secure local job opportunities and reduce average commuting distance.
- The location, as far as possible, of new settlements and other major developments along railway corridors to secure the best possible public transport access to other major centres.
- The development at regional level of long-term investment strategies for integrated public transport, using resources which would otherwise be spent on new roads.

New business developments:

- The development of new policy guidelines for the location of businesses and public offices (together with suitable parking standards), with the aim of minimising total commuting mileages – such policies, which could perhaps be developed along the lines of the Dutch 'right business in the right place' strategy, might then be set out in a future planning policy guidance note.
- The introduction of mileage reduction plans, to be developed and implemented by businesses and public organisations within government-issued guidelines and supported through financial incentives.

Shopping:

- Continued strong support for city and town centre shopping (with new development permitted only where it reinforces existing provision) and for the maintenance of local shopping facilities.
- Major new retail developments to be subjected to a full shopping impact analysis, which would include an assessment of the traffic likely to be generated, both in terms of the absolute numbers of vehicles and total vehicle mileage, and an assessment of the public transport provision.

Table 6.6 *Continued*

Accessibility to schools:

- Requirements on local planning and education authorities to place maximum emphasis on safe routes to school by foot, by bicycle and by public transport, and to ensure that new primary schools in urban areas are generally no more than a 5 minute walk away from the children's homes.
- A requirement upon highway and education authorities, together with the schools concerned, to carry out comprehensive reviews of the adequacy of public transport and school buses servicing secondary schools, with a view, where necessary, to reorienting spending programmes to upgrade these services.
- The publication of an advice and good practice guide for local authorities on the development of safe routes to school, and the allocation of some initial central funding for such schemes.

Access to local facilities:

- Commitments through local planning policies to secure a full range of local facilities which are readily accessible by foot or bicycle, both in new residential areas and, when the opportunity arises, in older ones.
- The planning of future residential areas of any significant size around high-quality public transport routes, with homes generally no more than a 5 minute walk away from a bus or light-rail stop.

Integrated transport strategies at the urban level:

- A requirement upon those responsible for land use and transport planning within our major cities to prepare integrated transport strategies, the aims of which would include the development of high-quality public transport services, significant reductions in overall vehicle emissions and, generally, a vastly improved environment for those who live and work there.

Source: Hall (1993: 12).

widely used in developed countries is the differential pricing of petrol through the level of taxation it attracts, to reduce the use of leaded petrol and to increase the consumption of unleaded petrol. A more radical solution advocated by the EC is the introduction of a carbon tax on energy production so that more environmentally sound sources are developed to reduce pollution. Yet this has been fiercely resisted by governments such as the UK's because they feel it would add additional costs to the price of energy and thereby increase the costs of production. The basis of their argument is that for tourist transport it could lead to an uncompetitive effect for UK transport operators on a global basis. In this respect, concerted international government action is needed with certain countries taking a lead while others are forced to follow suit through international pressure, to reduce levels of pollution from transport. For example, in the UK the deregulation of bus services in metropolitan areas has led to new operators using aged vehicles which contribute higher levels of pollution compared with the former metropolitan Passenger Transport Executives (PTEs) where grants were provided to update fleets, thereby using more energy-efficient vehicles (Knowles and Hall 1992). Yet as Button and Rothengatter (1992) acknowledge, the global nature of transports' impact on the environment is likely to intensify. The implementation of sustainable transport policies needs to be accompanied by changes in the lifestyles of tourists so that they recognise the environmental degradation which their process of travel induces.

Good practice in sustainable tourist transport

The real debate over achieving sustainable tourist transport options is usually focused on the outcome: can such options really be put in practice or do they remain a stated policy objective of environmental planning which is little more than a paper exercise? There are various examples of good practice cited in the tourism literature where transport is a core component of tourism planning, so that conservation and interpretation of the environment raises tourists' awareness of natural habitats and the need for a delicate balance to be achieved between tourist use and preservation. The Tarka Project in Devon is one example where a tourism strategy has achieved these objectives (see English Tourist Board/Employment Department 1991 for more details). However, the reliance on public and private sector transport operators to implement sustainable tourism is questioned by Wood and

House (1991, 1992). Although Wood and House (1991) acknowledge that transport operators need to pursue good environmental practices, they also advocate that the onus should also be placed on the tourist. Their central argument is that tourists should 'environmentally audit themselves' before and during their holiday and this principle could also be applied to aspects of business travel. The environmental audit is based on a number of simple questions:

- Why go on holiday? – consider your motivations and whether you really need to travel.
- Choose the right type of holiday to meet your needs.
- Consider travelling out of season to less well-known destinations.
- Choose the right travel method and tour operator after asking environmentally related questions in relation to what the company is doing to minimise environmental impacts.
- Consider the form of transport you will use getting to the point of departure.
- Does the tour operator contract transport companies with new, energy-efficient vehicles and aircraft or are they old, noisy and less efficient?
- Is public transport, cycling (Scottish Tourist Board 1991) or walking a feasible option when you are at the destination as opposed to hiring a car?

Wood and House's (1992) book *The Good Tourist in France* illustrates how tourists can make their trip sensitive to the environment, especially in their use of transport. Wood and House (1992) provide information on 'how to get there' but more importantly they undertake detailed research on each region of France so that tourist travel in the destination area can be based on sustainable options (i.e. forms of transport which do not have major environmental impacts). They outline details of operators and locations where you can hire or purchase travel services based on:

- rail travel
- bus/coach travel
- car travel
- boating
- cycling
- walking
- riding

as well as contact addresses of local groups which encourage and support sustainable development. How can one evaluate the extent to which sustainable tourism and tourist travel are realistic propositions in the 1990s?

The evaluation of sustainable principles for tourist transport

During the 1980s the concept of mass tourism came under greater scrutiny as a range of influential books questioned whether the economic benefits of tourism were adequately compensating for the increasing environmental impact. This was followed by the development of 'sustainable', 'responsible', 'green' or 'soft' tourism, and a growing recognition that tourism cannot easily be managed where the carrying capacity (see Pigram 1993 for a discussion of this term) of the environment is greatly exceeded. The development of marketing strategies with 'sustainable' in their title has emerged as a response to this interest in the environment, but all too often the strategies have failed to grasp the carrying capacity and absolute numbers of tourists which different locations can support. Consequently tourist transport has contributed to growing pressure on tourism environments by the provision of services to locations that have outgrown their carrying capacity. Therefore, it is not surprising to find criticisms of the sustainable tourism movement which has been manipulated by certain commercial interests as a new trend they can use to sell tourism and transport services to the more discerning and environmentally aware tourists.

Wheeler (1992a) argues that it is difficult to visualise sustainable tourism as a realistic solution for tourism as the world is now experiencing 'megamass tourism' which is viewed as the next stage on from mass tourism. While sustainable tourism (Wheeler 1992b) is emphasising small-scale individual tourist activities at specific locations and the substitution of the term traveller for tourist, a rather elitist movement has developed, supported by a small number of more 'progressive tourists'. Herein lies a major contradiction in the sustainable debate: the insatiable demand for tourist travel is incompatible with the rather up-market, small-scale and expensive form of tourism which only a limited number of tourists are likely to afford. As a concept, sustainability is still in its early stages of development and is unlikely to lead to major changes in the tourist transport system, being more appropriate as a marketing tool for 'new tourism' (Poon 1989). In all probability sustainable tourist travel cannot be achieved until the concept has been researched further and the fundamental problem of megamass tourism is addressed.

Although the design of resort areas and man-made tourist attractions able to meet the demands of megamass tourism may be able to deal with the high throughput of tourists in a restricted geographical area (e.g. Disneyland) there will be a growing demand for tourist transport to reach these artificial and synthetic tourism environments. This may have a temporary effect in reducing pressure on other, more fragile tourism environments while the needs of tourists are met by these staged tourist attractions. But the real prospect of environmental damage will emerge if mass tourism trends are based on the search for a more authentic experience (MacCannel 1976). The fundamental problem of environmental impacts is likely to remain and future techno-logical advances may offer a lifeline for the environment, if staged tourism can be developed further for the mass tourist using new ideas such as 'virtual reality' to meet the tourists' need for entertainment, excitement and pleasure.

As tourist transport operations are usually characterised by private sector ventures, voluntary agreements have typically been the basis for environmental management policies. Government organisations can assist in this process by ensuring that legislation is in place to encourage a reduction in environmental pollution from transportation. Govern-ment commitment to sustainable transport policies in developed countries seems to have foundered as the decision to deregulate trans-port is unlikely to see such options implemented given the reliance on profitability in tourist transport provision rather than environmental issues. Pigram (1993) argues that in the process of policy formulation and implementation of sustainable tourism options, it is important to recognise the role of major decision-makers such as transport operators in influencing the long-term success of such schemes. Ultimately, the tourists' desire for international and domestic travel may need to be the focus of long-term educational strategies to identify some of the prob-lems travel, tourism and transport pose for the environment. One radical solution may be to increase the cost of travel and introduce government regulations to restrict the demand, to reduce the impact on the environment. Yet there are many political and ethical objections to such an approach since it is reminiscent of the situation in some Eastern European countries before the collapse of communist rule and it would be tantamount to an infringement of individual freedom in democratic societies. Increasing the cost and restricting the opportunity to travel has other social implications because it may run contrary to the objectives of social tourism which aims to make travel and holidays accessible to all social groups. A partnership approach between responsible transport and tour operators and governments committed to making tourists more aware of their own actions may be one way forward. Rather than regulating tourist travel, tourists should be encouraged to exercise greater restraint in their demand for travel, though it is evident that there is no short-term solution to obviating the environmental impact of tourist transport systems.

Summary

The human effects and environmental consequences of tourist transport have led to a greater awareness of how tourist transport systems interact with the human and physical environment. The concept of 'sustainable tourism has burdened itself with incompatible conflicting objectives – small scale sensitivity and limited numbers to be achieved in tandem with economic viability and significant income and employment impacts' (Wheeler 1991: 95). In other words, sustainable tourism's implicit assumption that smaller-scale tourist activities will result from such developments could pose threats to the economic threshold at which tourist travel services are provided. If sustainable tourism is viewed as the only legitimate form of tourism, it would have unrealistic social impacts by limiting travel to a privileged minority which:

> appeases the guilt of the thinking tourist while simultaneously providing the holiday experience they or we want. The industry is happy because the more discerning (and expensive) range of market can be catered for by legitimately opening up new areas to tourism.
>
> (Wheeler 1991: 96)

This highlights the rather superficial nature of the sustainability concept which does not really offer any long-term solutions to the tourist and the transport provider because it fails to address the global impact of tourism, which is too large a problem for governments and transport operators to address in isolation. Even if tourist transport providers and tour operators withdrew from carrying tourists to sensitive environments, the competitive nature of tourist transport provision in market economies would mean that another rival operator, with less interest in environmental issues, may enter the market. Environmental auditing and EA are moving the transport business towards considering the consequences of transporting tourists to different environments, but the reliance on private sector co-operation in minimising their impact may only result in action:

> where the benefits [of environmental auditing] are largely enjoyed by third parties or the general public . . . [but] . . . if consumers' current search for quality embraces an increasing environmental awareness, the tourism industry would face demand-led pressure to adopt environmental auditing more widely.
>
> (Goodall 1992: 73)

Questions

1 Why do tourists travel?
2 What problems do they encounter when travelling?
3 Can you distinguish between environmental assessment and environmental auditing? In what context would these techniques of environmental research be used in tourist transport systems?
4 To what extent can tourist transport be developed in a sustainable framework?

Further reading

Barde, J.P. and Button, K.J. (eds) (1990) *Transport Policy and the Environment: Six Case Studies*, London: Earthscan.

Budowski, G. (1976) 'Tourism and environmental conservation: conflict, coexistence or symbiosis?', *Environmental Conservation* 3, 1: 27–31.

Farrington, J. and Ord, D. (1988) 'Bure Valley Railway: an EIA', *Project Appraisal* 3, 4: 210–18.

Hoyle, B.S. and Knowles, R.D. (eds) (1992) *Modern Transport Geography*, London: Belhaven (especially pp. 51–66).

7
Tourist transport systems and service provision in the 1990s

This book aims to raise awareness of the relationship between tourism and transport by developing the concept of a tourist transport system as a means of analysing the processes shaping the provision and consumption of transport services by tourists. Throughout the book, transport is emphasised as a dynamic and active element in the tourist's experience of travelling because it is a vital part of the process of tourism. Some of the first-generation tourism textbooks (e.g. Mathieson and Wall 1982) regarded tourist transport as an essential part of tourism but it was not worthy of study in its own right.

Although there is not space within this introductory book to undertake a comprehensive review of transport for tourism, it has sought to focus on how the consumer, provider and other agencies (e.g. national governments) interact in different transport systems. The concept of a tourist transport system was developed as a framework in which to understand the inter-relationships between different elements in such systems. Using a systems approach to the analysis of tourist transport also highlighted the importance of inputs to the system (e.g. the demand and supply) as well as controlling influences (e.g. government policy) and outputs (the tourist travel experience) and the effect on the environment. The book has also sought to identify a number of processes which characterise the tourist transport system. For example, deregulation is a process now affecting tourist transport systems in North America, Western Europe and Australasia (Button 1991) as well as communist states such as China (Taplin 1993). Within the existing literature, the discussion of tourist transport systems has remained fragmented and dependent upon generalised empirical or extremely specialised studies of both tourism and transport. The interface between tourism and transport has not been integrated into a holistic framework. Whilst tourism is now regarded as a complex phenomenon by educators and researchers, its frequent association with transport has meant that social science researchers have failed to integrate these issues in a framework where the complementarity between tourism and transport could be explored further. The tendency within tourism research to focus on typologies of tourism and tourists has led to a critical separation of tourists from the mode of transport they use. This has the effect of contributing to the separation of tourism and transport research, where tourist motivation to travel is viewed in isolation from the process of travelling. The result is tourist travel divided into two discrete elements (transport and the tourist) rather than being conceptualised as a continuous process using a systems approach. How can our understanding of tourist transport systems be developed further in the 1990s?

In Chapters 1 and 2, the scope of multidisciplinary research on tourism and transport is reviewed in terms of the concepts and methods of each discipline (economics, geography and marketing) used to analyse tourist transport. However, the different philosophical backgrounds of researchers from these disciplines mean that their approach to tourist transport is not easy to synthesise into a holistic framework. Moreover, the tendency for researchers to retain their disciplinary training in economics, geography or marketing has simply contributed to the growing body of knowledge on transport and tourism. For our understanding of tourist transport systems and the tourist's experience of travel to develop a greater degree of coherence and a theoretical basis, research will need to be interdisciplinary in nature requiring greater collaboration among researchers. Interdisciplinary research requires people from different disciplines to collaborate and focus on a specific research problem, where different questions are asked about the topic without each researcher losing sight of the problem under consideration. This may help to integrate the contributions which different disciplines can make to the analysis of tourist transport systems to achieve a more holistic understanding of the operation, management and use of transport services by tourists.

Tourist transport systems are likely to be affected by various opportunities and constraints on tourist travel in the 1990s. For example, congestion of airspace in developed countries such as North America and Western Europe will remain a persistent problem for policy-makers and transport planners in the 1990s. At the same time the demand for long-haul travel in developed countries is set to expand in the 1990s which may pose opportunities for transport providers and tour operators if constraints can be overcome. Environmental issues will also feature more prominently in tourist transport systems as a new generation of travellers, familiar with green issues in the 1980s, emerge as consumers of tourist transport services. Understanding the relative importance of these factors in shaping the tourist's desire to travel on different modes of transport will be a major challenge for service providers, as the sustainability debate (see Weiler 1993) focuses on more environmentally sensitive and novel modes of transport.

Increasingly the patronage of tourist transport services is going to depend upon the ability of providers to differentiate their services on the basis of image, market positioning and reputation for service quality. The 1990s are emerging as the decade of the consumer in relation to tourist travel, with providers responding to legitimate requests for higher standards of comfort, reliability and courtesy as part of the travel experience. Passengers are now recognised as customers and their rights and needs are beginning to gain a higher profile in the provision, quality and management of tourist transport services. Is this concern with service quality a passing phase or is it part of a more deep-rooted trend associated with service provision in contemporary society?

Enhancing the tourist's travel experience: service quality and total quality management

Throughout this book reference is made to service provision as a process and the term quality appears in various contexts. Why has this issue been raised in various guises throughout the book? It is widely acknowledged that the 1980s saw that many service providers in North America responded to a perceived 'quality' crisis posed by products and services offered by rivals in the Pacific Rim (Deming 1982). Many service providers responded with corporate strategies focused on quality issues as a means of addressing the perceived threat of higher-quality services and products supplied by rivals as a method of retaining market share. Yet if the late 1980s were characterised by a business environment committed to quality, the early 1990s are dominated by total quality management (TQM) as a more sophisticated form of recognising customers' needs as an integral part of an organisation's goals. TQM developed as a corporate business management philosophy and it even has an academic journal – *Total Quality Management* – devoted to research in this area. Why should this be of interest to the tourist transport system in the 1990s? The growing concern for consumers, quality and total supply management in the tourist transport system is part of the move towards TQM among service providers. Furthermore, TQM is likely to assume a greater role in academic and commercial research on tourist transport in the 1990s.

TQM is one all-embracing approach which enables an organisation to develop a more holistic view of consumers, quality issues and service provision as an ongoing process. Yet one of the principles of TQM – the concern for quality – is explicitly dealt with in detail in this book. One reason for this concerns the difficulty of establishing a universal definition of quality which could be applied to tourist transport systems. Dotching and Oakland (1992) provide an excellent review of this issue, citing the work by Townsend and Gebhart (1986) which distinguishes between the subjective evaluation of quality by the customer (quality of perception) and the provider's more objective assessment (quality of fact). Clearly the meaning of quality will vary according to the context and perception of who is establishing what can be deemed as quality. While the journal of TQM contains many interesting discussions of this issue, operationalising TQM in a tourist transport context requires organisations to work towards specific goals focused on an agreed concept of quality. Corporate commitment is required so that TQM permeates all areas of the company's business. TQM also provides an organisation with the opportunity to monitor and implement internal procedures and to control suppliers using established quality standards such as BS 5750, as discussed in Chapter 6.

One of the real challenges for TQM in tourist transport systems is to establish what the customer considers as excellence in service provision and the design of service delivery systems to deal with individual tourist's requests, requirements and needs. Many corporations involved in tourist transport provision are trying to make individual tourists feel more valued as customers but, until delivery systems are able to deal fully with this issue, operators will be unable to claim success in TQM. It is at the strategic policy and planning stage that organisations may need to agree on how to improve continuously and strive for quality in service provision so that the tourist's travel experience is enhanced. One challenge is to ensure that the process of travel is not perceived as such a mundane and stressful experience for some tourists.

Implementing a TQM strategy is no easy task for organisations where it may involve a change in corporate culture. Nevertheless, a number of critical factors characterise success in TQM in service provision. As Table 7.1 shows, senior management set on developing a policy for TQM will need to follow certain principles and management strategies if they seriously wish to embrace and succeed in TQM. Porter and Parker (1992) note that management behaviour and their willingness to carry through such programmes is often the key to the successful implementation of TQM.

However, the interest in TQM is no substitute for the organisational and logistical skills involved in co-ordinating and managing tourist transport systems. Conveying large numbers of people over short and long distances for pleasure and business is a complex process requiring a great deal of planning and organisation on a day to day basis as well as in the longer term. Adding a concern for quality provision in this process makes the delivery of services a more complex undertaking and it is not surprising that service interruptions occur due to the sheer volume and scale of people handled in tourist transport systems. But when things do go wrong, companies and their front-line staff must be empowered to deal with incidents or systems must be in place to deal with crises when they occur.

Government policy, planning and investment in infrastructure assume a significant role in facilitating the efficient movement of people for the purpose of tourism. In this context, the London Tourist Board's (1990) 'At the Crossroads: The Future of London's Transport' reaffirms the essential relationship between transport and tourism dealt with in Chapter 1. The London Tourist Board study is quite unique in this respect since it recognised that:

- An efficient transport network is necessary for tourists to gain access to a destination such as London; without a transport network tourism would not exist as it is part of the tourism infrastructure.
- An integrated transport network with convenient transfers between different modes of transport is essential with reasonably priced travel options.
- Within the destination, tourists need a choice of transport to transfer between the port of arrival and their final destination.
- Investment in public transport provides social, economic and environmental benefits for both residents and tourists alike. Investment in transport infrastructure is a long-term proposition and is unlikely

Table 7.1 Implementing a total quality management programme

Senior management in an organisation seeking to implement a TQM programme should consider the following:

- an organisation needs long-term commitment to constant improvement
- a culture of 'right first time' is required
- employees need to be trained to understand customer–supplier relationships
- purchasing practices need to consider more than just the price – they must also consider the total cost
- improvements in delivery systems need to be managed
- the introduction of modern methods of supervision and training need to be explained to avoid fear and intransigence
- breaking down inter-departmental barriers by managing the service process to improve communications and teamwork
- eliminating
  - goals without methods
  - standards based only on numbers
  - fiction: get facts by using the correct tools (e.g. by using appropriate research techniques)
- developing an ongoing human resource management strategy to develop experts and 'gurus'
- developing a systematic approach to managing the implementation of TQM.

The implementation of a TQM programme can be shaped using these principles to achieve OUTCOMES, which involves:

- the identification of customer–supplier relationships
- managing processes
- cultural changes
- commitment

which may need to be accompanied by management necessities including:

- systems based on international standards
- teams to monitor and improve quality throughout the systems
- tools to analyse and predict what type of corrective action is needed to improve quality.

Source: Modified from Dotching and Oakland (1992: 142).

to yield tangible benefits in market-led economies in relation to tourism. Yet without it, tourism would not be able to develop.

As the London Tourist Board study notes, the development and long-term prosperity of tourism depends on transport both to make destinations accessible and to facilitate tourist travel within the destination area. Efficiency, safety and ease of travel and convenient interchanges are likely to be viewed as important performance indicators by users of tourist transport systems. These principles apply to the wider context of tourist travel and for providers; making the travel experience more rewarding is one major challenge for all parties involved in tourist transport systems in the 1990s.

Questions

1 How does a systems approach help researchers to understand the issue of service quality in tourist transport provision?
2 To what extent does interdisciplinary research offer a way forward to understanding the functioning, operation and management of tourist transport systems?
3 What is total quality management?

Further reading

Berry, L.L. and Parasuraman, A. (1991) *Marketing Services: Competing Through Quality*, New York: The Free Press.
Fitzsimmons, J.A .and Sullivan, R.S. (1982) *Service Operations Management*, New York: McGraw Hill.
Townsend, P.L. and Gebhart, J.E. (1986) *Commit to Quality*, New York: John Wiley.
Zeithmal, A. and Berry, L.L. (1985) 'A conceptual model of service quality and its implications for future research', *Journal of Marketing* Fall: 41–50.

Select bibliography

Adams, J. (1981) *Transport Planning: Vision and Practice*, London: Routledge and Kegan Paul.

Adamson, M., Jones, W. and Platt, R. (1991) 'Competition issues in privatisation: lessons for the railways', in D. Banister and K.J. Button (eds) *Transport in a Free Market Economy*, Basingstoke: Macmillan: 49–78.

Allen, D. and Williams, G. (1985) 'The development of management information to meet the needs of a new management structure', in K.J. Button and D. Pitfield (eds) *International Railway Economics: Studies in Management and Efficiency*, Aldershot: Gower: 85–100.

Annals of Tourism Research (1991) 'Special issue: Tourism Social Science', *Annals of Tourism Research* 18, 1.

Anon (1992) 'Japan', *International Tourism Reports* 4: 5–35.

Archdale, G. (1991) 'Computer Reservation Systems – the international scene', *Insights* November: D15–20.

Archer, B.H. (1987) 'Demand forecasting and estimation', in J.R.B. Ritchie and C.R. Goeldner (eds) *Travel, Tourism and Hospitality Research: A Handbook for Managers and Researchers*, New York: John Wiley: 77–85.

—— (1989) 'Tourism and small island economies', in C.P. Cooper (ed.) *Progress in Tourism, Recreation and Hospitality Management Volume 1*, London: Belhaven: 125–35.

Ardill, J. (1987) 'The environmental impact', in B. Jones (ed.) *The Tunnel: The Channel Tunnel and Beyond*, Chichester: Ellis Horwood: 177–212.

Banister, D. (1992) 'Policy responses in the UK', in D. Banister and K.J. Button (eds) *Transport, the Environment and Sustainable Development*, London: E and FN Spon: 53–78.

Banister, D. and Button, K.J. (eds) (1991) *Transport in a Free Market Economy*, Basingstoke: Macmillan.

—— (1992) *Transport, the Environment and Sustainable Development*, London: E and FN Spon.

Banister, D. and Hall, P. (eds) (1981) *Transport and Public Policy Planning*, London: Mansell.

Barbier, E.B. (1988) *New Approaches in Environmental and Resource Economics: Towards an Economics of Sustainable Development*, London: International Institute for Environment and Development.

Barke, M. (1986) *Transport and Trade*, Edinburgh: Oliver and Boyd.

Baum, T. (ed.) (1993) *Human Resource Issues in International Tourism*, Oxford: Butterworth–Heinemann.

Beesley, M.E. (1989) 'Transport research and economics', *Journal of Transport Economics and Policy* 23: 17–28.

Bell, G., Blackledge, D. and Bowen, P. (1983) *The Economics of Transport and Planning*, London: Heinemann.

Berry, L.L. and Parasuraman, A. (1991) *Marketing Services: Competing Through Quality*, New York: The Free Press.

Bird, P. and Rutherford, B.A. (1989) *Understanding Company Accounts*, London: Pitman.

Bitner, M.J. (1992) 'Servicescapes: the impact of physical surroundings on customers and employees', *Journal of Marketing* 56, 2: 57–71.

Bitner, M.J., Booms, B.H. and Tetreanit, M.S. (1990) 'The service encounter: diagnosing favourable and unfavourable incidents', *Journal of Marketing* 1: 71–84.

Bote Gómez, V. and Sinclair, M.T. (1991) 'Integration in the tourism industry: a case study approach', in M.T. Sinclair and M.J. Stabler (eds) *The Tourism Industry: An International Analysis*, Wallingford: CAB International: 67–90.

British Airways (1992) *Annual Environmental Report*, Hounslow: British Airways.

British Railways Board (1992) *The British Rail Passenger's Charter*, London: British Railways Board.

British Tourist Authority (1991) *1993 Cross-Channel Marketing Strategy*, London: British Tourist Authority.

Britton, S. (1982) 'The political economy of tourism in the Third World', *Annals of Tourism Research* 9, 3: 331–58.

Buckley, P.J. (1987) 'Tourism – an economic transaction analysis', *Tourism Management* 8, 3: 190–4.

Buckley, P.J. and Casson, M. (1985) *The Economic Theory of the Multinational Enterprise: Selected Papers*, London: Macmillan.

Bull, A. (1991) *The Economics of Travel and Tourism*, London: Pitman.

Burkart, A. and Medlik, S. (1974) *Tourism, Past, Present and Future*, Oxford: Heinemann.

—— (eds) (1975) *The Management of Tourism*, Oxford: Heinemann.

Bus and Coach Council (1991) *Buses and Coaches: The Way Forward*, London: Bus and Coach Council.

Button, K.J. (1982) *Transport Economics*, London: Heinemann.

—— (1990) 'The Channel Tunnel – economic implications for the South East', *Geographical Journal* 156, 2: 87–99.

—— (1991) *Airline Deregulation: International Experiences*, London: Fulton.
Button, K.J. and Gillingwater K. (eds) (1983) *Future Transport Policy*, London: Routledge.
Button, K.J. and Rothengatter, W. (1992) 'Global environmental degradation: the role of transport', in D. Banister and K.J. Button (eds) *Transport, the Environment and Sustainable Development*, London: E and FN Spon: 19–52.
Bywater, M. (1990) 'Japanese investment in South Pacific tourism', *Travel and Tourism Analyst* 3: 51–64.
Cannon, T. (1989) *Basic Marketing Principles and Practice*, Third Edition, London: Holt, Rinehart and Winston.
CEDRE (1990) *Transports à grande vitesse: développement régional et ménagement du territoire, rapport de synthèse*, Strasbourg: Centre Européen du Développement Régional.
Channel Tunnel Group (1985) *The Channel Tunnel Project: Environmental Effects in the UK*, London: Channel Tunnel Group.
Channel Tunnel Joint Consultative Committee (1986) *Kent Impact Study*, London: Department of Transport.
Chou, Y.H. (1993) 'Airline deregulation and nodal accessibility', *Journal of Transport Geography* 1, 1: 36–46.
Clift, S. and Page, S.J. (eds) *Health and the International Tourist*, London: Routledge, forthcoming.
Coase, R. (1937) 'The nature of the firm', *Economica* 4: 386–405.
Cohen, E. (1972) 'Towards a sociology of international tourism', *Social Research* 39: 164–82.
Collier, A. (1989) *Principles of Tourism*, Auckland: Longman Paul.
Cossar, J., Reid, D., Fallon, R., Bell, E., Riding, M., Follett, E., Dow, B., Mitchell, S. and Grist, N. (1990) 'A cumulative review of studies of travellers, their experience of illness and the implications of these findings', *Journal of Infection* 21: 27–42.
Cowell, D.W. (1986) *The Marketing of Services*, London: Heinemann.
Craven, J. (1990) *Introduction to Economics*, Second Edition, Oxford: Blackwell.
David, F.R. (1989) 'How companies define their mission statements', *Long Range Planning* 22, 1: 90–7.
Deming, W.E. (1982) *Quality Productivity and Competitive Position*, Cambridge, MA: Massachusetts Institute of Technology.
Department of the Environment (1989) *Environmental Assessment: A Guide to the Procedures*, London: HMSO.
—— (1991) *This Common Inheritance*, London: HMSO.
Department of Statistics (1992) *New Zealand Official 1992 Yearbook: 95th Edition*, Wellington: Department of Statistics.
Department of Transport (1987) *Tourism, Leisure and Roads*, London: HMSO.
—— (1992a) *New Opportunities for the Railways, Cm 2012*, London: HMSO.
—— (1992b) *The Franchising of Passenger Rail Services: A Consultative Document*, London: Department of Transport.
—— (1993) *Railways Bill 1993: Bill 117*, London: HMSO.
Dickinson, R. (1993) 'Cruise industry outlook in the Caribbean', in D.J. Gayle

and J.N. Goodrich (eds) *Tourism Marketing and Management in the Caribbean*, London: Routledge: 113–21.

Doganis, R. (1992) *The Airport Business*, London: Routledge.

Dotching, J.A. and Oakland, J.S. (1992) 'Theories and concepts in Total Quality Management', *Total Quality Management* 3, 2: 133–45.

Eadington, W.R. and Redman, M. (1991) 'Economics and tourism', *Annals of Tourism Research* 18, 1: 41–56.

Edwards, A. (1991) *European Long Haul Travel Market: Forecasts to 2000*, London: Economist Intelligence Unit.

—— (1992) *Long Term Tourism Forecasts to 2005*, London: Economist Intelligence Unit.

English Tourist Board/Employment Department (1991) *Tourism and the Environment: Maintaining the Balance*, London: English Tourist Board.

European Conference of Ministers of Transport (1992) *Privatisation of Railways*, Brussels: European Conference of Ministers of Transport.

Eurostat (1987) *Transport, Communications, Tourism*, Luxembourg: Office for Official Publication of the European Communities.

Farrington, J.H. (1985) 'Transport geography and policy – deregulation and privatisation', *Transactions of the Institute of British Geographers* 10, 1: 109–19.

—— (1992) 'Transport, environment and energy', in B.S. Hoyle and R.D. Knowles (eds) *Modern Transport Geography*, London: Belhaven: 51–66.

Faulks, R. (1990) *Principles of Transport*, Fourth Edition, Maidenhead: McGraw-Hill.

Flipo, J. (1988) 'On the intangibility of services', *Service Industries Journal* 8, 3: 286–98.

Forer, P.C. and Pearce, D.G. (1984) 'Spatial patterns of package tourism in New Zealand', *New Zealand Geographer* 40, 1: 34–42.

Foster, D. (1985) *Travel and Tourism Management*, London: Macmillan.

Gant, R. and Smith, J. (1992) 'Tourism and national development planning in Tunisia', *Tourism Management* 13, 3: 331–6.

Gayle, D.J. and Goodrich, J.N. (eds) (1993) *Tourism Marketing and Management in the Caribbean*, London: Routledge.

Gibb, R. and Charlton, C. (1992) 'International surface passenger transport: prospects and potential', in B.S. Hoyle and R.D. Knowles (eds) *Modern Transport Geography*, London: Belhaven: 215–32.

Gilbert, D.C. (1989) 'Tourism marketing – its emergence and establishment', in C.P. Cooper (ed.) *Progress in Tourism, Recreation and Hospitality Management Volume 1*, London: Belhaven: 77–90.

—— (1990) 'Conceptual issues in the meaning of tourism', in C.P. Cooper (ed.) *Progress in Tourism, Recreation and Hospitality Management Volume 2*, London: Belhaven: 4–27.

—— (1991) 'An examination of the consumer behaviour process related to tourism', in C.P. Cooper (ed.) *Progress in Tourism, Recreation and Hospitality Management Volume 3*, London: Belhaven: 78–105.

Gilbert, D.C. and Joshi, I. (1992) 'Quality management and the tourism and hospitality industry', in C.P. Cooper and A. Lockwood (eds) *Progress in*

Tourism, Recreation and Hospitality Management Volume 4, London: Belhaven: 149–68.

Glaister, S. (1981) *Fundamentals of Transport Economics*, Oxford: Blackwell.

Glaister, S. and Mulley, C.M. (1983) *Public Control of the Bus Industry*, Aldershot: Gower.

Go, F. and Murakami, M. (1990) 'Transnational corporations capture Japanese travel market', *Tourism Management* 11, 4: 348–58.

Golich, V.L. (1988) 'Airline deregulation: economic boom or safety bust', *Transportation Quarterly* 42: 159–79.

Goodall, B. (1991) 'Understanding holiday choice', in C.P. Cooper (ed.) *Progress in Tourism, Recreation and Hospitality Management Volume 3*, London: Belhaven: 58–77.

— (1992) 'Environmental Auditing for tourism', in C.P. Cooper and A. Lockwood (eds) *Progress in Tourism, Recreation and Hospitality Management Volume 4*, London: Belhaven: 60–74.

Goodenough, R. and Page, S.J. (1993) 'Tourism training and education in the 1990s', *Journal of Geography in Higher Education* 17 1: 57–75.

— (1994) 'Evaluating the environmental impact of a major transport infrastructure project: the Channel Tunnel rail-link', *Applied Geography* 14, 1: 26–50.

Government of Ireland (1990) *Operational Programme on Peripherality: Roads and Other Transport Infrastructure 1989–1993*, Dublin: Stationery Office.

Graham, A. (1992) 'Airports in the United States', in R. Doganis *The Airport Business*, London: Routledge: 188–206.

Griffith, L. (1989) 'Airways sanctions against South Africa', *Area* 21, 3: 249–59.

Gronroos, C. (1980) *An Applied Service Marketing Theory*, Working Paper No.57, Helsinki: Sweden School of Economics and Business Administration.

Gunn, C.A. (1988) *Tourism Planning*, Second Edition, New York: Taylor and Francis.

Hall, C.M. (1991) *Introduction to Tourism in Australia: Impacts, Planning and Development*, Melbourne: Longman Cheshire.

Hall, D. (1993) 'Getting around – transport and sustainability', *Town and Country Planning* 62, 1/2: 8–12.

Halsall, D. (1992) 'Transport for tourism and recreation', in B.S. Hoyle and R.D. Knowles (eds) *Modern Transport Geography*, London: Belhaven: 155–77.

Hamilton, J. (1988) 'Trends in tourism demand patterns in New Zealand', *International Journal of Hospitality Management* 7, 4: 299–320.

Hay, A. (1973) *Transport for the Space Economy: A Geographical Study*, London: Macmillan.

Henshall, D., Roberts, R. and Leighton, A. (1985) 'Fly–drive tourists: motivation and destination choice factors', *Journal of Travel Research* 23, 3: 23–7.

Heraty, M.J. (1989) 'Tourism transport – implications for developing countries', *Tourism Management* 10, 4: 288–92.

HMSO (1978) *Airports Policy*, London: HMSO.

— (1990) *International Passenger Survey*, London: HMSO.

Hodgson, P. (1991) 'Market research in tourism: how important is it?', *Tourism Management* 11, 4: 274–7.

Hoivik, T. and Heiberg, T. (1980) 'Centre–periphery tourism and self reliance', *International Social Science Journal* 32, 1: 69–98.

Holder, J.S. (1988) 'Pattern and impact of tourism on the environment of the Caribbean', *Tourism Management* 9, 2: 119–27.

Holliday, I., Marcou, G. and Vickerman, R. (1991) *The Channel Tunnel: Public Policy, Regional Development and European Integration*, London: Belhaven.

Holloway, J.C. (1989) *The Business of Tourism*, Third Edition, London: Pitman.

Holloway, J.C. and Plant, R.V. (1988) *Marketing for Tourism*, London: Pitman.

Horner, A. (1991) 'Geographical aspects of airport and air-route development in Ireland', *Irish Geography* 24, 1: 35–47.

Hoyle, B.S. and Knowles, R.D. (eds) (1992) *Modern Transport Geography*, London: Belhaven.

Humphries, B. (1992) 'The air transport market', *INSIGHTS* September: A37–42.

Hunt, J. (1988) 'Airlines in Asia', *Travel and Tourism Analyst* 5: 5–25.

Javalgi, R.G., Thomas, E.G. and Rao, S.R. (1992) 'U.S. pleasure travellers' perceptions of selected European destinations', *European Journal of Marketing* 26, 1: 46–64.

Jefferson, A. and Lickorish, L. (1988) *Marketing Tourism: A Practical Guide*, Harlow: Longman.

Jemiolo, J. and Oster, C.V. (1981) 'Regional changes in airline service since deregulation', *Transportation Quarterly* 41: 569–86.

Johnson, P. (1988) 'The impact of a new entry on UK domestic air transport: a case study of the London–Glasgow route', *Service Industries Journal* 8, 3: 299–316.

Kihl, M. (1988) 'The impacts of deregulation on passenger transportation in small towns', *Transportation Quarterly* 42: 27–43.

Killen, J. and Smith, A. (1989) 'Transportation', in R.W.G. Carter and A.J. Parker (eds) *Ireland: A Contemporary Geographical Perspective*, London: Routledge: 271–300.

Knowles, R.D. (ed.) (1985) *Implications of the 1985 Transport Bill*, Salford: Transport Geography Study Group, Institute of British Geographers.

—— (1989) 'Urban public transport in Thatcher's Britain', in R.D. Knowles (ed.) *Transport Policy and Urban Development: Methodology and Evaluation*, Salford: Transport Geography Study Group, Institute of British Geographers.

—— (1993) 'Research agendas in transport geography for the 1990s', *Journal of Transport Geography* 1, 1: 3–11.

Knowles, R.D. and Hall, D.R. (1992) 'Transport policy and control', in B.S. Hoyles and R.D. Knowles (eds) *Modern Transport Geography*, London: Belhaven: 11–32.

Kotler, P. and Armstrong, G. (1991) *Principles of Marketing*, Fifth Edition, Englewood Cliffs, NJ: Prentice Hall.

Land Use Consultants (1986) *The Channel Fixed Link: Environmental*

Appraisal of Alternative Proposals: A Report prepared for the Department of Transport, London: HMSO.

Latham, J. (1989) 'The statistical measurement of tourism', in C.P. Cooper (ed.) *Progress in Tourism, Recreation and Hospitality Management Volume 1*, London: Belhaven: 55–76.

—— (1992) 'International tourism statistics', in C.P. Cooper and A. Lockwood (eds) *Progress in Tourism, Recreation and Hospitality Management Volume 4*, London: Belhaven: 267–73.

Lavery, P. (1989) *Travel and Tourism*, First Edition, Huntingdon: Elm.

Laws, E. (1991) *Tourism Marketing: Service and Quality Management Perspectives*, Cheltenham: Stanley Thornes.

Laws, E. and Ryan, C. (1992) 'Service on flights – issues and analysis by the use of diaries', *Journal of Travel and Tourism Marketing* 1, 3: 61–71.

Lawton, L.J. and Butler, R.W. (1987) 'Cruise ship industry – patterns in the Caribbean 1880–1986', *Tourism Management* 8, 4: 329–43.

Lee, N. and Wood, C. (1988) 'The European Directive on environmental assessment: implementation at last?', *The Environmentalist* 9, 3: 177–86.

Leiper, N. (1990) *Tourism Systems: An Interdisciplinary Perspective*, Palmerston North: Massey University, Department of Management Systems, Occasional Paper 2.

Lew, A. (1991) 'Scenic roads and rural development in the U.S.', *Tourism Recreation Research* 16, 2: 23–30.

Lickorish, L.J., in association with Jefferson, A., Bodlender, J. and Jenkins, C.L. (1991) *Developing Tourism Destinations: Policies and Perspectives*, Harlow: Longman.

Lipsey, R.G. (1989) *An Introduction to Positive Economics*, London: Weidenfeld and Nicolson.

London Tourist Board (1990) *At the Crossroads: The Future of London's Transport*, London: London Tourist Board.

Lovelock, C. (1992a) 'Seeking synergy in service operations: seven things marketers need to know about service operations', *European Management Journal* 10, 1: 22–9.

—— (1992b) *Managing Services: Marketing, Operations and Human Resources*, Second Edition, Englewood Cliffs, NJ: Prentice Hall.

Lowe, J.C. and Moryadas, S. (1975) *The Geography of Movement*, Boston: Houghton Mifflin.

Lundberg, D.E. (1980) *The Tourist Business*, New York: Van Nostrand Reinhold.

MacCannel, D. (1976) *The Tourist: A New Theory of the Leisure Class*, New York: Schocken Books.

McIntosh, I.B. (1989) 'Travel considerations in the elderly', *Travel Medicine International*: 69–72.

—— (1990a) 'The stress of modern travel', *Travel Medicine International*: 118–21.

—— (1990b) 'Travel sickness', *Travel Medicine International*: 80–3.

McIntosh, R.W. and Goeldner, G.R. (1990) *Tourism: Principles, Practices and Philosophies*, New York: John Wiley.

Mann, J.M. and Mantel, C.F. (1992) 'Travel and health: a global agenda',

Travel Medicine Two, Proceedings of the Second International Conference on Travel Medicine, Paris: 1–4.

Mansfeld, Y. (1992) 'Tourism: towards a behavioural approach', *Progress in Planning* 38, 1: 1-92.

Mathieson, A. and Wall, G. (1982) *Tourism: Economic, Physical and Social Impacts*, Harlow: Longman.

Middleton, V.T.C. (1988) *Marketing in Travel and Tourism*, London: Heinemann.

Mill, R.C. (1992) *Tourism: The International Business*, Second Edition, Englewood Cliffs, NJ: Prentice Hall.

Mill, R.C. and Morrison, A.M. (1985) *The Tourism System: An Introductory Text*, Englewood Cliffs, NJ: Prentice Hall.

Monopolies and Mergers Commission (1989) *Cross-Channel Car Ferries*, Cm 584, London: HMSO.

Moore, A. (1985) 'Japanese tourists', *Annals of Tourism Research* 12, 4: 619–43.

Morean, B. (1983) 'The language of Japanese tourism', *Annals of Tourism Research* 10, 2: 93–109.

Morris, S. (1990) *Japanese Outbound Travel Market in the 1990s*, London: Economist Intelligence Unit.

Morrison, S. and Winston, C. (1986) *The Economic Effects of Airline Deregulation*, Washington, DC: Brookings Institution.

Moses, L.N. and Savage, I. (1990) 'Aviation deregulation and safety: theory and evidence', *Journal of Transport Economics and Policy* 14: 171–88.

Murphy, P.E. (1985) *Tourism: A Community Approach*, London: Routledge.

National Consumer Council (1991) *Consumer Concerns 1990*, London: National Consumer Council.

—— (1992) *British Rail Privatisation*, London: National Consumer Council.

Newson, M. (1992) 'Environmental economics, resources and commerce', in M. Newson (ed.) *Managing the Human Impact on the National Environment: Patterns and Processes*, London: Belhaven: 80–106.

Nozawa, H. (1992) 'A marketing analysis of Japanese outbound travel', *Tourism Management* 13, 2: 226–34.

O'Kelly, M.E. (1986) 'The location of interacting hub facilities', *Transportation Science* 20, 2: 92–106.

Ortuzar, J. de D. and Willumsen, L. E. (1990) *Modelling Transport*, Chichester: John Wiley.

Page, S.J. (1989a) 'Changing patterns of international tourism in New Zealand', *Tourism Management* 10, 4: 337–41.

—— (1989b) 'Tourist development in London Docklands in the 1980s and 1990s', *GeoJournal* 19, 3: 291–5.

—— (1989c) 'Tourism planning in London', *Town and Country Planning* 58, 3: 334–5.

—— (1992a) 'The ferries and the Channel Tunnel', *Travel Industry Monitor* 23: 11.

—— (1992b) 'Managing tourism in a small historic city', *Town and Country Planning'*, 61, 7–8: 208–11.

—— (1992c) 'Perspectives on the environmental impact of the Channel Tunnel on tourism', in C.P. Cooper and A. Lockwood (eds) *Progress in Tourism, Recreation and Hospitality Management Volume 4*, London: Belhaven: 82–102.

—— (1993a) 'Urban tourism in New Zealand: the National Museum of New Zealand Project', *Tourism Management* 14, 3: 211–17.

—— (1993b) 'Tourism and peripherality: a review of tourism in the Republic of Ireland', in C.P. Cooper (ed.) *Progress in Tourism, Recreation and Hospitality Management Volume 5*, London: Belhaven, 26–53.

—— (1993c) 'Waterfront revitalisation in London: market-led planning and tourism in London Docklands', in S. Craig-Smith and M. Fagence (eds) *Urban Waterfront Development: An International Survey*, New York: Praeger, in press.

—— (1993d) 'European rail travel', *Travel and Tourism Analyst* 1: 5–30.

—— (1993e) 'Editorial highlight: the Channel Tunnel', *Tourism Management*, 14, 6: 419–23.

—— (1994) 'Editorial: the spatial implications of the Channel Tunnel', *Applied Geography* 14, 1: 3–8.

Page, S.J. and Sinclair, M.T. (1992a) 'The Channel Tunnel: an opportunity for London's tourism industry', *Tourism Recreation Research* 17, 2: 57–70.

—— (1992b) 'The Channel Tunnel and tourism markets', *Travel and Tourism Analyst* 1: 8–32.

Pearce, D.G. (1979) 'Towards a geography of tourism', *Annals of Tourism Research* 6, 3: 245–70.

—— (1985) 'Tourism and environmental research: a review', *International Journal of Environmental Studies* 25, 4: 247–55.

—— (1987) *Tourism Today: A Geographical Analysis*, Harlow: Longman.

—— (1990) *Tourist Development*, 2nd edn, 2nd rpt, Harlow: Longman.

—— (1992) *Tourism Organisations*, Harlow: Longman.

Pearce, D.G. and Butler, R.W. (eds) (1993) *Tourism Research: Critiques and Challenges*, London: Routledge.

Pearce, D.G. and Elliot, J.M. (1983) 'The Trip Index', *Journal of Travel Research* 22, 1: 6–9.

Pearce, P.L. (1982) *The Social Psychology of Tourist Behaviour*, Oxford: Pergamon.

Peisley, T. (1992a) *World Cruise Ship Industry in the 1990s*, London: Economist Intelligence Unit.

—— (1992b) 'Ferries, short sea cruises and the Channel Tunnel', *Travel and Tourism Analyst* 4: 5–26.

Perkins, H.C. and Cushman, G. (eds) (1993) *Leisure, Recreation and Tourism*, Auckland: Longman-Paul.

Peters, T.J. and Waterman, R.H. (1982) *In Search of Excellence*, London: Harper and Row.

Pigram, J.J. (1993) 'Planning for tourism in rural areas: bridging the policy implementation gap', in D.G. Pearce and R.W. Butler (eds) *Tourism Research: Critiques and Challenges*, London: Routledge: 156–74.

Polunin, I. (1989) 'Japanese travel boom', *Tourism Management* 10, 1: 4–8.

Poon, A. (1989) 'Competitive strategies for a new tourism', in C.P. Cooper (ed.) *Progress in Tourism, Recreation and Hospitality Management Volume 4*, London: Belhaven: 91–102.

Porter, L.J. and Parker, A.J. (1992) 'Total Quality Management – the critical success factors', *Total Quality Management* 4, 1: 13–22.

Potter, S. (1987) *On the Right Lines: The Limits of Technological Innovation*, London: Pinter.

Prideaux, J. (1990) 'InterCity: passenger railway without subsidy', *Royal Society of Arts Journal*, March: 244–54.

Qaiters, C.G. and Bergiel, B.J. (1989) *Consumer Behaviour: A Decision-Making Approach*, Delaware, OH: South Western Publishing.

Reid, D. and Cossar, J. (1993) 'Epidemiology of travel', *British Medical Bulletin* 49, 2: 257–68.

Romeril, M. (1985) 'Tourism and the environment – towards a symbiotic relationship', *Journal of Environmental Studies* 25: 215–18.

—— (1989) 'Tourism and the environment – accord or discord?', *Tourism Management* 10, 3: 204–8.

Ross, W.A. (1987) 'Evaluating environmental impact statements', *Journal of Environmental Management* 25: 137–47.

Ryan, C. (1991) *Recreational Tourism: A Social Science Perspective*, London: Routledge.

Schiffman, L.G. and Kanuk, L.L. (1991) *Consumer Behaviour*, Fourth Edition, Englewood Cliffs, NJ: Prentice Hall.

Scottish Tourist Board (1991) *Tourism Potential of Cycling and Cycle Routes in Scotland*, Edinburgh: Scottish Tourist Board.

Sealy, K. (1992) 'International air transport', in B.S. Hoyle and R.D. Knowles (eds) *Modern Transport Geography*, London: Belhaven: 233–56.

Seibert, J.C. (1973) *Concepts of Marketing Management*, New York: Harper Row.

Selman, P. (1992) *Environmental Planning: The Conservation and Development of Biophysical Resources*, London: Paul Chapman.

SERPLAN (1989) *The Channel Tunnel: Impact on the South East*, London: SERPLAN.

SETEC/Wilbur Smith Associates (1989) *Review of Market Trends and Forecasts*, Paris: Eurotunnel.

Sharpley, R. (1993) *Tourism and Leisure in the Countryside*, Huntingdon: Elm.

Shaw, S. (1982) *Airline Marketing and Management*, London: Pitman.

Shaw, S.L. (1993) 'Hub structures of major US passenger airlines', *Journal of Transport Geography* 1, 1: 47–58.

Shilton, D. (1982) 'Modelling the demand for high speed train services', *Journal of Operational Research Society* 33: 713–22.

Sikorski, D. (1990) 'A comparative evaluation of the government's role in national airlines', *Asia Pacific Journal of Management* 7, 1: 97–120.

Simmons, D. and Leiper, N. (1993) 'Tourism: a social science perspective', in H. C. Perkins and G. Cushman (eds) *Leisure, Recreation and Tourism*, Auckland: Longman-Paul: 204–20.

Sinclair, M.T. (1991) 'The economics of tourism', in C.P. Cooper (ed.) *Progress in Tourism, Recreation and Hospitality Management Volume 3*, London: Belhaven: 1–27.

Sinclair, M.T. and Page, S.J. (1993) 'The Euroregion: a new framework for regional development', *Regional Studies* 27, 5: 475–83.

Sinclair, M.T. and Stabler, M. (1991) 'New perspectives on the tourism industry', in M.T. Sinclair and M.J. Stabler (eds) *The Tourism Industry: An International Analysis*, Wallingford: CAB International: 1–14.

Singapore International Airlines (1992) *Singapore International Airlines Annual Report 1991–92*, Singapore: Singapore International Airlines.

Smith, M.J.T. (1989) *Aircraft Noise*, Cambridge: Cambridge University Press.

Smith, S.L.J. (1989) *Tourism Analysis*, Harlow: Longman.

Smith, V.L. (1992) 'Boracay, Philippines: a case study in alternative tourism', in V.L. Smith and W.R. Eadington (eds) *Tourism Alternatives: Potential and Problems in the Development of Tourism*, Philadelphia: Pennsylvania University Press: 133–57.

Smith, V.L. and Eadington, W. R. (eds) (1992) *Tourism Alternatives: Potential and Problems in the Development of Tourism*, Philadelphia: Pennsylvania University Press.

Sommerville, H. (1992) 'The airline industry's perspective', in D. Banister and K.J. Button (eds) *Transport, the Environment and Sustainable Development*, London: E and FN Spon: 161–74.

Starkie, D.N. (1976) *Transportation Planning, Policy and Analysis*, Oxford: Pergamon.

Steward, S. (1986) *Air Disasters*, London: Arrow Books.

Stubbs, P.C., Tyson, W.J. and Dalvi, M. (1980) *Transport Economics*, London: Allen and Unwin.

Taafe, E.J. and Ganthier, H.L. (1973) *Geography of Transportation*, Englewood Cliffs, NJ: Prentice Hall.

Taplin, J.H.E. (1993) 'Economic reform and transport policy in China', *Journal of Transport Economics and Policy* 27, 1: 75–86.

TEST (1991) *The Wrong Side of the Tracks*, London: TEST.

Teye, W.B. (1992) 'Land transportation and tourism in Bermuda', *Tourism Management* 13, 4: 395–405.

Therivel, R.B. and Barret, B.F.D. (1990) 'Airport development and E.I.A.: Kansai International Airport, Japan', *Land Use Policy* 7, 1: 80–6.

Thornberry, N. and Hennessey, H. (1992) 'Customer care, much more than a smile: developing a customer service infrastructure', *European Management Journal* 10, 4: 460–4.

Todd, G. and Mather, S. (1993) *Tourism in the Caribbean*, London: Economist Intelligence Unit.

Tokuhisa, T. (1980) 'Tourism within, from and to Japan', *International Social Science Journal* 32, 1: 128–50.

Tourism Society (1990) *Tourism and the Environment: A Memorandum to the Department of Employment Task Force*, London: The UK Tourism Society.

Townsend, P.L. and Gebhart, J.E. (1986) *Commit to Quality*, New York: John Wiley.

Turton, B. (1991) 'The changing transport pattern', in R.J. Johnston and V. Gardiner (eds) *The Changing Geography of the British Isles*, Second Edition, London: Routledge: 171–97.

—— (1992a) 'British Rail passenger policies', *Geography* 77, 1: 64–7.

—— (1992b) 'Inter-urban transport', in B.S. Hoyle and R. Knowles (eds) *Modern Transport Geography*, London: Belhaven: 105–24.

United States Bureau of the Census (1992) *Statistical Abstract of the United States: 1992*, 112th Edition, Washington, DC: United States Bureau of Census.

Usyal, M. and Crompton, V.L. (1985) 'An overview of approaches used to forecast tourism demand', *Journal of Travel Research* 23, 4: 7–15.

Van Dierdonck, R. (1992) 'Success strategies in a service economy', *European Marketing Journal* 10, 3: 365–73.

Veal, A. (1992) *Research Methods in Leisure and Tourism*, Harlow: Longman.

Viant, A. (1993) 'Enticing the elderly to travel – an exercise in Euromanagement', *Tourism Management* 14, 1: 52–60.

Wales Tourist Board (1992) *Infrastructure Services for Tourism – A Paper for Discussion*, Cardiff: Wales Tourist Board.

Wathern, P. (1990) *Environmental Impact Assessment: Theory and Practice*, London: Unwin Hyman.

Weiler, B (1993) 'Guest Editor's Introduction', *Tourism Management* 14, 2: 83–4.

Wheeler, B. (1991) 'Tourism: troubled times', *Tourism Management* 12, 2: 91–6.

—— (1992a) 'Is progressive tourism appropriate?', *Tourism Management* 13, 1: 104–5.

—— (1992b) 'Alternative tourism – a deceptive ploy', in C.P. Cooper and A. Lockwood (eds) *Progress in Tourism, Recreation and Hospitality Management Volume 4*, London: Belhaven: 140–6.

White, H.P. and Senior, M.L. (1983) *Transport Geography*, Harlow: Longman.

Whitelegg, J. (1987) 'Rural railways and disinvestment in rural areas', *Regional Studies* 21, 1: 55–64.

Wilkinson, P.F. (1989) 'Strategies for tourism in island microstates', *Annals of Tourism Research* 16, 2: 153–77.

Williams, P.W. (1987) 'Evaluating environmental impact on physical capacity in tourism', in J.R.B. Ritchie and C.R. Goeldner (eds) *Travel, Tourism and Hospitality Research: A Handbook for Managers and Researchers*, New York: John Wiley: 385–97.

Witt, S.F., Brooke, M.Z. and Buckley, P.J. (1991) *The Management of International Tourism*, London: Unwin Hyman.

Witt, S.F. and Martin, C. (1989) 'Demand forecasting in tourism and recreation', in C.P. Cooper (ed.) *Progress in Tourism, Recreation and Hospitality Management Volume 1*, London: Belhaven: 4–32.

—— (1992) *Modelling and Forecasting Demand in Tourism*, London: Academic Press.

Witt, S.F. and Moutinho, L. (eds) (1989) *Tourism Marketing and Management Handbook*, Hemel Hempstead: Prentice Hall.

Wood, K. and House, S. (1991) *The Good Tourist*, London: Mandarin.

—— (1992) *The Good Tourist in France*, London: Mandarin.

World Commission on the Environment and Development (1987) *Our Common Future* (Bründtland Commission's Report), Oxford: Oxford University Press.

World Tourism Organisation (1992) *Yearbook of Tourism Statistics*, Madrid: World Tourism Organisation.

Yardley, L. (1992) 'Motion sickness and perception: a reappraisal of the sensory conflict approach', *British Journal of Psychology* 82: 449–71.

Zeithmal, A. and Berry, L.L. (1985) 'A conceptual model of service quality and its implications for future research', *Journal of Marketing* Fall: 41–50.

Subject index

geographical concepts to analyse tourist transport 23–4
geography 10, 23, 44
Greyhound Bus operations 51

hub and spoke system 27
human consequences of tourist travel 139–45; preflight anxieties 140–1; airside problems 140–1; transmeridian disturbance 140–1; fears and phobias 140–1; psychological concerns 140–2; measures to reduce stress 143–4

International Civil Aviation Organisation 73, 151
International Passenger Survey 84
international tourism trends 71–3
international tourist arrivals: New Zealand 17; Tunisia 81

Japanese outbound travel 85–95; airport development 92–3; data sources 87; evolution of demand 89–91; expansion of demand 87–8; government policy 88–9; prospects for the 1990s 94–5; Ten Million Programme 93, 98

load factor 21–2

macroeconomics 12, 22
marketing 10, 44; cross-Channel tourist travel 33–8; definition 30; mix 30, 40–1; research 30, 38–9; tourist transport 29–44
microeconomics 11
mission statement 32
Monopolies and Mergers Commission 37–8
monopoly 22

national product 11
nodes 28
noise pollution 151, 153

oligopoly 22
Organisation for Economic Cooperation and Development 75–6, 82, 98

P & O European Ferries 36; BS 5750 148
Passenger's Charter 63–5
price elasticity 14
production 11

service quality 178–82
services: as a process 42; consumer benefit 43; core elements 41; inseparability 41; intangibility 41; perishability 41; service concept 42–3; service delivery system 42, 44; service encounter 42, 44; service offer 42–4
spokes 27
Stena Sealink 36, 38
strategic planning 30–3
supply of tourist transport services 20–2, 100–38; customer questionnaire used by Thomson Holidays 108; integration 105–19; integration in Singapore International Airlines 116; Lunn Poly travel agencies 106–7; quality control systems 107–8; Thomson Holidays 108; Total Supply Management 106; transaction analysis 102–5
supply of tourist transport in destination areas 130–6
sustainable tourism 145
sustainable tourist-transport systems 164–74; evaluation of sustainable principles 172–4; good practice 170–2; implementation 167–70; policy-making 166–7
SWOT analysis 33, 36–7
systems approach 4–5

Total Quality Management 178–82
tourism and the environment 146–8
tourism forecasting 95–8; Delphi method 96
tourism geography and tourist transport 27–9
tourism product 13
tourism statistics: European Community sources 83; International Passenger Survey 84
tourism studies 2–4
tourism system 5–6
tourist experience 4
tourist transport as a service 2–4, 41–4, 101–2, 176–82
tourist transport system 4, 6, 9, 130–6; an analytical framework 4
tours 28–9
transport and the environment 145–6
transport and tourism, relationship between 2–6
transport geography concepts: catchments 24; hierarchy of airports 25, 27; hub and

Place index

존재
수필
333.8 4761